MEMÓRIA

MEMÓRIA

An Anthology of Portuguese Canadian Writers

Edited by Fernanda Viveiros

Foreword by Onésimo T. Almeida

Fidalgo

Library of Congress Preassigned Control Number (PCN) is on file.

ISBN 978-0-9860565-0-5

Published in the United States by Fidalgo Books

Printed and bound in Canada by Friesens

Interior page design by Jan Westendorp / Kato Design & Photo
Cover photograph, *Sunset over São Miguel*, by Gaspar Avila
Cover design by Jane Jeszeck, Jigsaw / www.jigsawseattle.com

The text is set in Albertan, designed by Jim Rimmer (1934–2010) and originally used for hand-setting and printing limited-edition books at his private press and foundry in New Westminster, B.C. He named the typeface after his wife, Alberta.

Fidalgo Books
www.fidalgobooks.com

CONTENTS

ONÉSIMO T. ALMEIDA

A Foreword, or sort of

A foreword to an anthology of Portuguese Canadian authors by a Portuguese in America requires some explaining (to some Canadians, perhaps an apology would be more appreciated). Thus, I might as well handle it at the start.

I have heard many times that, after hockey, national identity is the greatest Canadian conversation topic. I am also aware of the fact that the struggle for Canadian identity is not vis-à-vis the United Kingdom, but the United States—the huge, threatening elephant with which Canada shares a bed (the Mexicans are said to complain about their dismal fate, "So far from God and so close to the United States!"). In spite of such awareness, I still accepted the kind invitation to write a foreword for this Portuguese Canadian literary anthology where I will claim that, all Canadian wishes for differentiation from the United States notwithstanding, for all practical purposes the Portuguese Canadian communities are osmotically connected to their Portuguese American counterparts, belonging as they do to the same cultural world. That is why I usually collapse both under the general denomination of Portuguese **North** American communities ("North" being intentionally stressed). Supported by the contemporary conversation on hybridity, I contend that the Portuguese communities in Canada and the United States can hardly be told apart, at least for now. Their people come from basically the same places of origin, the Azores and rural mainland Portugal. There are many divided families, with members—brothers and sisters, parents, children—living some in the Northern and others in the Southern side of the international frontier. There is an intense traffic between both sides, a perennial border crossing in both directions, particularly between the provinces of Ontario-Québec and New England. Relatives and friends visit each other for religious feasts as well as for happy family occasions such as weddings, baptisms, graduations and vacations, or sad ones like illnesses and deaths. I often repeat that if one could watch on the screen of a computer the cars loaded with Portuguese Americans and Portuguese Canadians travelling on Interstate 90 on any given weekend, one would be able to see a continuous line.

Obviously, I am calling attention to all this in order to stress the idea of a common cultural ground shared by the Portuguese of the United States and Canada. Still, with the communities in the United States being much older, it is only natural that a literary expression started to emerge there much earlier than in Canada.

Things are changing rapidly, however, and the present volume is a good sign in that respect. The texts gathered here are written by authors who have had, and many still have, strong ties to the Portuguese Canadian community. They speak as insiders, often struggling to maintain a healthy balance between the old world of their parents and their own new, broader, vaster one, the latter not rarely in deep conflict with the former. Without presuming to be sociological or anthropological works, these writings are literary dives into the milieu in which their authors grew up, hence the mark of truthfulness that so clearly transpires from these pages. The reader enters a complex nest of inner conflicts between old and modern values, insecure identities, rejections and strong affections, and hard choices between old loyalties and appealing novelties.

My reader may rightly remind me that this is nothing new, that it is after all common to any ethnic writing in the United Sstates and Canada or, for that matter, in any part of the world. True. With one specificity, though: in entering these pages I can immediately identify a very particular universe, genuinely Portuguese as seen by Portuguese eyes, yet through special lenses as if looking in from the outside. Why do I say this? In trying to answer such question I feel as challenged as the philosopher David Hume when asked to define identity, *If I am asked to do it, I cannot, but there is no doubt I will never confuse it with anything else.*

The answer, therefore, must be found in the pages of this book, in meeting with its lively authors and characters, in listening to their engaging voices. None of them have attained yet the literary recognition of, say, Anthony De Sa or Erika de Vasconcelos, but it is nevertheless a rich, polyhedric collection, attaining unity despite a rather diverse set of texts, including poetry of very different styles and traditions.

I started by establishing a connection between the Portuguese American and the Portuguese Canadian communities, and I will conclude with another connection also close to home. In his piece about his place in Canada, one writer seems to be referring to my own world in New England. Like him, having witnessed in the past cultural conflicts of Portuguese immigrants with their American neighbors who were against the raising of animals such as chickens in the backyards, now I also have ecologically concerned urbanites raising chickens and bees next door (with big green flies coming around, in spite of all their technologically sophisticated hygienic cares). I will not quote the author for I don't wish to take the pleasure of reading his cute remark in its proper context from the reader.

That, however, is just one of the many charming notes that this collection has to offer. There are numerous others to be found.

PROVIDENCE, RHODE ISLAND

FERNANDA VIVEIROS

Preface

What value is there in collecting the work of a small group of writers on the basis of ethnicity alone? The answer is as simple as proposing a celebration, a recognition of the emerging literary contributions of Portuguese Canadians, a community which celebrated the 60th anniversary of its en masse immigration to Canada earlier this year. It would also be true to say that this anthology was born in part of a sense of responsibility to add the voices of Portuguese Canadians to the multicultural chorus heard across this nation.

The Portuguese voyagers of old spread canticles, proverbs, ballads, moral tales, chivalric prose, drama, and the lives of saints all over the world. From Camões to Eça de Queirós to Pessoa and Saramago, the Portuguese are as renowned for their literature as for their seagoing explorations. However, for the Portuguese who landed on Canada's shore, there was little time to dwell on words. Immigration was the beginning of a hard life, albeit in community, as they sacrificed their own dreams to build new lives for their families. The voices of the first generation were unheard; their words forgotten, ignored, lost. I'd like to think I'm paying homage to their stories and memories with the publication of this book.

This slender volume of prose and poetry is a testament to the emergence of Portuguese Canadian literature, with more of our words and stories being brought to the attention of more people than ever before. In "Coastal poem," Eduardo Bettencourt Pinto writes, "*My voice races towards you—never has it flown like this, so high over the world.*" Portuguese Canadian literature is flying, quietly, through its own discovery.

In the call for submissions I was careful not to set too many limits to the subject matter or the style of fiction to be submitted; as a result, the editorial board was rewarded with an interesting and diverse collection of pieces ranging from poems and folktales to memoir extracts and short stories. We read stories from those most deeply entrenched in the challenges of ethnic identity to those who seem to have transcended them. As much as we tried to be inclusive, we had to make difficult decisions to leave out many writers whose work intrigued us. In the end, we chose fifteen Portuguese Canadian writers of greater and lesser acclaim whose work best illustrated a wide range of experiences, narrative voices and sensibilities.

I am grateful to those who so enthusiastically contributed their time and talent. Special thanks to my editorial board, professors Maria João Dodman and Hugh Hazelton, who supported my vision and guided the selection process. I would like to thank Professor Hazelton for also generously sharing his expertise as a translator, and Dr. Irene Marques for her proofreading of the Portuguese text.

This anthology is dedicated to Canadians of Portuguese ethnicity, a community I am proud to call my own. I hope the collection of writing within this book widens the realm of possibility for Portuguese Canadian writers and offers insight into who we are as individuals, as members of an all-too-silent ethnic group and more importantly, as the keepers of memories for those who come after us.

SEPTEMBER 2013

PAULO DA COSTA

ser português

é nascer com o fado ao pescoço

        viver de olhos ancorados
        ao alto mar, ansiar pela maré
        de partir ou pela onda do regresso

        viver enlatado entre mar e espanha
                exportar sardinhas

        ir à missa e esquecer o sermão

é confessar-se a amigos
de garrafa na mão

é não fazer ondas
bastam as que revoluteiam no mar

        rezar pela paz
        admirar fátima e batalha
        na mesma santa visita

        ser português é

        amar o carro mais que a si próprio

é bastante mais em conta

        ser português é

to be portuguese

is to be born with the *fado* around your neck

> to live with your eyes anchored
> to the open sea, longing for the outgoing tide
> or for its incoming wave

> living canned up between the sea and spain
> exporting sardines

> going to mass and forgetting the sermon

it's confessing to friends
with a bottle in your hand

and not making waves
the ones that stir up the sea are enough

> praying for peace
> admiring fátima and batalha
> in the same holy visit

> to be portuguese is

> to love your car more than yourself

and find it more affordable

> to be portuguese is

partir para o estrangeiro josé
e regressar joe

ser pequeno
mas de grande olho

ser português é

não ser castelhano

nascer com dores ali, pobrezinho, viver
com dores aqui do lado, senhor doutor,
e morrer com dores acolá, valha-nos deus

é oferecer o peito do churrasco aos filhos
afugentando a fome própria com asas raquíticas

deixar o ninho de barbas brancas

ser português é

não ser nada disto
mas ámen

é discutir política
como quem discute futebol

abrir a porta da garrafeira e da salgadeira
a estranhos - aferrolhar a janela da mente

ser português é

imortalizar poetas e heróis que inflacionam o ego
desta nação de pueris e fictícios orgulhos

to travel abroad josé
and come back joe

to be small
but with an eye for everything

to be portuguese is

not to be spanish

to be born with pains in there, poor thing, living
with pains right here in my side, doctor,
and dying with pains over there, god help us

it's offering the barbecued chicken breast to the kids
fighting off your own hunger with a few puny wings

leaving the nest when your whiskers are white

to be portuguese is

not to be any of this
but to say amen to it all

it's discussing politics
the way you discuss soccer

opening the doors of the wine-cellar and salted meats
to strangers—bolting the window of the mind

to be portuguese is

to immortalize the poets and heroes that inflate the ego
of this nation of naïve fictitious pride

D. Henrique, o navegador que jamais navegou, Fernão
Magalhães o primeiro circum-navegante que jamais regressou

ser embalado por histórias grandiosas e
imperialistas de especiarias e conquistas

obcecado pela nódoa nos colarinhos
desleixado para com as nódoas na história

ser português é

esquecer as redes de destruição
que varreram o mar até ao silêncio

encadeados pelo brilho da idade de ouro
minimizar as violações, degolações, genocídios

gitano, judeu, a escravidão do tráfego, extirpar urso, lince,
bacalhau, águia-imperial, abutre quebra-ossos

é fazer do leito azedo
queijo fresco

esquecer que o mar tudo devolve
até os séculos indigeríveis

ser português é

engolir a isca camoniana
da escola até à morte

não permitir que a sua perspectiva de um só olho
finalmente se afogue na profundidade da memória

Prince Henry, the navigator who never set sail, Fernando
Magellan, the first man to go round the world and never return

to get wrapped up in grandiose imperialist
histories of the search for spices and conquests

obsessed with a stain on the collar
ignoring the stains on history

to be portuguese is

to forget about the fishnets of destruction
that swept the sea to silence

chained to the gleam of the golden age
minimizing the rapes, beheadings, genocides

gypsies, jews, the slave trade, eradicating bears, lynx,
cod, imperial eagles, bearded vultures

it's turning sour milk
into fresh cheese

forgetting that the sea spews back everything
even the indigestible centuries

to be portuguese is

to swallow the camonian bait
from school to death

not letting his one-eyed perspective
drown in the depths of memory

é ceder à tentação da carne, das coxas,
da lagosta, das rabanadas
e ter barriga para tudo

é partilhar
a última nesga de broa

é legar uma herança de sonhos incompletos
envelhecer danado ou calado

       esperar que os herdeiros lhes concluam os passos

é pensar que no estrangeiro tudo é melhor
mas nada existe que chegue aos calcanhares
do nosso presunto, praias ou broa

       ser português é

é suspirar que o copo de tinto
se encontra meio vazio

       sentar-se à espera que aconteça
       que o mundo melhore, velhas desforras

       hipnotizado pela bola
       apanhado nas redes do jogo
       e no enredo da novela

       distrair-se enquanto o tinto se evapora

       ser português é

       ser licenciado em vítima

it's giving in to the temptations of the flesh, thighs,
lobster, French toast
and being able to stomach anything

sharing
the last piece of cornbread

leaving a legacy of unfinished dreams
growing old furiously or silently

          hoping your heirs will achieve your goals

and thinking that everything is better abroad
but nothing in the world ever measures up
to our smoked ham, beaches and cornmeal

        to be portuguese is

to sigh that the glass of red wine
is already half empty

        sitting down and waiting
        for the world to get better, to settle old scores

        hypnotized by the ball
        caught in the nets of the game
        or the plot of the soap opera

        getting distracted while the wine evaporates

        to be portuguese is

        to have a degree in being a victim

e a seu tempo em farmácia, direito,
assessor de balcão, engenheiro do desenrasca

é viver em imaculada limpeza e varrer
o lixo para a rua

é ser como qualquer outra nacionalidade
somente os pormenores diferem

é recolher cuidadosamente o plástico
que reveste o sofá
em honra da visita pascal do pároco

ser português é

torturar o touro, consciente
que as sortes o esperam
por trás de portas de morte privada
e acreditar que tal demonstra
um sinal de bom coração

sentir mais amor aos filhos
do que ao marido ou à esposa

acreditar que os jardins públicos e as florestas
não pertencem a ninguém

é examinar a fotografia da vida
pelo negativo

ser português é

ir-se andando, do mal o menos

and eventually in pharmacology, law,
as a shop-counter advisor, an engineer in getting by

it's living in immaculate cleanliness and sweeping
the trash out into the street

and being like any other nationality
differing only in the details

it's carefully removing the plastic
covering on the sofa
in honour of the parish priest's Easter visit

to be portuguese is

to torture the bull, knowing
the fate that awaits him
behind doors of private death
and believe this shows
how big-hearted you are

feeling more love for your children
than for your husband or wife

believing that public gardens and forests
don't belong to anyone

it's examining the photograph of life
through its negative

to be portuguese is

to go along from the lesser of two evils

poderia ser pior, seja o que Deus quiser

criticar tudo e todos, mas atenção
isto é uma via de sentido único

ser português é
escrever este poema

é conduzir o automóvel em perpétuo
estado de emergência

mais tarde ou mais medo
resulta mesmo em vítimas

culpar as estradas, o da frente
o de trás, os árbitros,
o vizinho do lado, seguido dos políticos,
por último o guarda-redes

é acreditar na palavra
erigir monumentos a poetas e ao redentor

ser português é

permanecer ou partir
mas carregar com tudo isto ao pescoço
como um crucifixo de ouro

it could be worse, if it's God's will

criticizing everything and everybody, but watch out
that's a one-way street

to be portuguese is
to write this poem

it's driving your car in a perpetual
state of emergency

more fear or later
there will always be victims

blaming the highways, the driver ahead
or the one behind, the referees,
the next-door neighbour, followed by the politicians,
and last of all the goal-keeper

and believing in the word
building monuments to poets and the redeemer

to be portuguese is

to stay or leave
but to carry all this around your neck
like a golden crucifix

TRANSLATED BY HUGH HAZELTON

EMANUEL MELO

Avó Lives Alone

Avó gets up at five in the morning to watch Portuguese Mass on television. She spends most of her day watching Portuguese soap operas and Portuguese news, but her favourite is always Mass. She watches two or three Masses throughout the day, but after the first early Mass she goes back to bed to sleep a bit more until maybe ten in the morning. She will have a late breakfast, and as soon as she has finished washing up the plate and cup and saucer, she will prepare her lunch, which she will eat at two o'clock. In between meals she will sit on the living room sofa to mend her granddaughters' socks or skirts or T-shirts.

"Bring everything to me," she begs her son, the girls' father. "It keeps me busy." And she will spend the quiet afternoons darning and sewing, her basket of threads and needles resting on the floor beside the sofa, while the television is on. Avó hardly watches shows in English anymore; not since her cable provider began to include foreign stations all the way from Portugal and Brazil. She will sit and watch until late at night and then start again with early Mass the next day. She feels grateful for the chance to watch television in her language; it allows her to be connected to her Portuguese roots in ways that were not possible when she first came to Canada decades ago when there were no Portuguese shows on Canadian television.

For dinner she organizes a tray with fruit, biscuits, cakes and yogurt, a small bit of chocolate, sometimes toast and a small recycled yogurt container full of peanuts or soy beans, salted, sometimes unsalted. She will then sit on her sofa with the tray on her lap and while she eats she will watch the evening shows. There's *O Preço Certo*, the Portuguese version of *The Price is Right*, and on Monday nights, *Prós e Contras*, a very interesting debates show where the host speaks with an erudite level of Portuguese that her *quarta classe* education did not prepare her for. The guest speakers use words she doesn't remember from her youth, technological and environmental words that were not even part of the vocabulary until recent times, and she attributes her lack of understanding to the fact that she has lived in Canada for too many decades of her life.

Every day she will try to call an old friend to chat for a bit or for an hour on the telephone. It breaks the silence of living alone. But every night she waits for her eldest son to call. "I knew it was you," she'll say through her chronic cough. Every time he calls her, there comes a loud cough through the receiver as he says, "Hello, *Mãe*." A long ripple of loud coughing continues until she says, "I don't understand why I cough so much but I've been doing it for years. It's a chronic thing."

Then she will tell him about the news and updates from the day. "Did you know that another young girl went missing today? Did you know that there was such a terrible storm in the Algarve? And a flood in the north?" Then, seamlessly, she mixes personal news with world news and in one breath tells him, "I had a hard time climbing the stairs after doing laundry this morning, my legs are no good, and there was a fire in the forests of Québec but I'm doing better now, *Graças a Deus*, oh, my God, I can't believe it, how mangled that car is and the bomb exploded right in front of those poor people . . ." Her son doesn't like to listen to the news but he'll sit quietly in his own home every night while he lets his mother ramble on. Sometimes she'll say how she hasn't spoken to anyone and how his is the first voice she has heard all day.

"Your cousin Berta made a beautiful vegetable soup. She brought some over for me today. She's a *querida*. I don't know what I would do without her. But Rita is also a *querida*. She's so patient and loves taking me grocery shopping when your brother's too busy. She never complains about doing a big shop for me, but your brother always complains that I put too much on my shopping list. I would go shopping more often but how can I bother your cousins so much?" Then, with hesitation in her voice, comes the real question she's been dying to ask.

"Have you spoken to your brother today?"

"No."

"Me too." He can hear the disappointed sadness in her tone.

"And how are *aquelas queridas*, my beautiful granddaughters?"

He will then let her know how he took his little nieces to the park to play on the swings or how he took them to a movie or went to their house for dinner. "They must be getting so tall," she says, hoping to know more about the little girls' progress. "Maybe your brother will bring them to see me the next time he does the grocery shopping for me."

Every six weeks, the girls' father receives a grocery list as long as a child's Santa Claus wish list before Christmas. He drives to No Frills and fills up boxes and more boxes of groceries. Sometimes the list is so long that he has to pay for one cartload of groceries, take them to the car, and then go back for a second load. When he arrives at Avó's house she doesn't pay attention to the groceries at first. All she can see is that her son has come alone this time and her smile fades into the content of the boxes as she scrutinizes them to make sure that he got the right brands and amounts of apples and oranges; everything must be precisely accounted for before she can ask.

"Sorry, Mãe. The girls are busy today. They have a birthday party to go to this afternoon." Other times it's their swimming lessons or ballet and skating that keep them away. "Ah, *paciência*." She lets out a sound of resignation over the disappointment of not seeing her granddaughters since Christmas. "*Fica para outra vez*." She comforts herself with the hope of a next time.

Her son puts away the groceries so that she doesn't have to. She watches him doing it, she tells him where things should go, he's still her little boy and she loves him very much. She loves both her sons but this one has given her grandchildren and he's the youngest and that makes him the more dear to her. For the grandchildren, she is grateful to him. After everything is quickly put away, there is no extra time for him to sit and talk or have something to eat; he hugs her goodbye and hurries back across town to his busy life. She watches his car disappear down the street, waving at it from behind her glass screen door, then closes the door, arms the house alarm, and goes back to sit down on her sofa.

"Ai, António, why did you leave me?" she asks the picture of her dead husband, the girls' Avô, who died a few years ago. That's when she began to live alone: after the brain cancer took her husband. But she likes her home, she feels safe in it, and likes having her things around her; the memories attached to photographs and mementos collected over a life time comfort her.

Everywhere she looks, something reminds her of a special time. "That sofa is where your father took his naps after he got sick. He loved to sleep when he wasn't reading the newspaper." She reminisces about her life when her oldest son comes for his weekly visit. She lives for the times when he comes to stay overnight. She spends the day making him special foods that she knows he'll like and by the time he arrives after work, she greets him at the door, tired but smiling, happy for his company, for the hug, for the human touch she's been without since his last visit. After dinner they watch the Portuguese shows together while eating *malasadas* with tea. They stay up late and in the morning, she makes him breakfast and prepares his lunch before he leaves, and always includes a big container of freshly-made vegetable soup for him to take home. She hugs him at the door and asks him for a big kiss. "Don't forget your poor mother," she tells him even though she knows that he will call her later in the evening. She watches him from behind her window until he waves back at her before getting on the bus. He always sees the shadow of her hand waving back and he knows that she is also smiling. Once he's out of sight, she turns around and goes back to sitting and praying and watching television for the rest of the day.

———

Avó gets bored easily. She doesn't get out much. Her arthritis, her difficulty in walking without losing balance, her weight, all keep her mostly house-bound until she has to go to a doctor's appointment or someone kindly takes her to church on Sundays. But it wasn't always like that. When Avô was alive and healthy they had a full and active life together. Even in retirement they found themselves very busy, especially when their first granddaughter was born. Avó and Avô looked upon the baby with huge smiles. It was the proudest day of their lives. How they fussed over her. "*Querida*," they whispered close to the baby's face, pouring their smiles into this newborn's life.

Once the baby's mother returned to work, the grandparents volunteered to babysit. Every weekday, early in the morning, the son or the daughter-in-law would drive across from the East End, where they lived, to drop off their precious baby in the West End, where the grandparents lived. Two years later, a second granddaughter was born. There was more joy, more pinching of cheeks and more *queridas* whispered into the new baby's ears. Soon, both girls were spending the days with their grandparents until their parents picked them up late at night. The older girl would take out all the pots and pans from the lower kitchen cabinets and spread them over the kitchen floor. There were toys scattered everywhere. And for Avó there was always laundry to do, soiled baby clothes to clean up, food to prepare. Avô did all the grocery shopping then.

"António," she would yell at him, "go get some *papo secos* at the bakery." When Avô returned, happy with his purchases at the end of completing all the errands his wife had sent him on for the day, she would look inside the brown paper bag full of oval buns and disapprovingly look at him as if he had just committed some crime. "I told you to get the round *papo secos*, not the long ones. What am I going to do with you?" And she'd make him go out again to get the buns she had specified. Avô was a patient, kind man. All his life he tried to make her happy, and no matter how unreasonable her demands, he strived to give her what she wanted.

When the workday came to an end, the girls' parents would arrive to bring them home. But first they would stay for dinner. "Thanks, Mãe, I don't know what we'd do without you," said the daughter-in-law as she kissed Avó before leaving. Both grandparents would stand by the door, watch the girls get strapped into their safety car seats and wave bye-bye as the car sped down the street. After the young family was gone and the house was quiet again from the joyful ruckus of the day, Avó and Avô tidied up, washed and dried the dishes, put them away and satisfied with the day, sat on the sofa together to watch television for the night. And so life went on like this for a few years, the girls growing taller each day. Sometimes, when the youngest grandchild arrived in the early morning, she would creep into the bedroom and, on tiptoe, approach the bed. "*Avô, Avô*, wake up." And startled into wakefulness, the grandfather would open his eyes and smile the biggest smile. "*Ah, a minha querida*," he'd say to her as he squeezed her into an embrace.

But then Avô got sick and the girls stopped coming over. Avó had too much to do now that she had to take care of her husband. Avô had lung surgery and he seemed to be better but then the doctors discovered that although his lungs were now fine, his brain wasn't so fine. "The spots have grown," informed the uncomfortable doctor. "There's not much more we can do, sorry." And the eldest son, who took Avô to all the doctor's appointments, had to translate the sad news into Portuguese. But how do you translate "you're going to die" in any language? You can't. So, the son simply took his father home.

Avô never complained about his cancer. He sat on the sofa, hiccupping for hours and hours, the side effects of medication he took as a last false hope but which left him worse off. Then, tired, he would lie down on the sofa, close his eyes, and sleep for the rest of the day.

"I miss *aquelas queridas filhas*," he would lament.

After a year, he became worse and within a few weeks gently died. That's when Avó began to live alone.

"Why don't you come and live closer to us?" begged her youngest son. "You could see the girls all the time; you'd be right beside us." But she couldn't bring herself to leave her home. It was all she had left to remind herself of the only man she'd ever loved, and of the life they had built together in Canada.

It took time but Avó has learned to adjust to being alone. She looks forward to Sunday mornings when a lady from church comes and drives her to Mass. Then she is brought back home to spend the rest of the day sitting quietly in the living room. She has her meals alone and always hopes that someone might stop by for a visit. She especially hopes her granddaughters will visit.

"*Graças a Deus*, I can still do things for myself," she says to her eldest son on the telephone. "Have you heard from your brother today?"

"No."

"Just asking . . . And how are my little granddaughters?"

———————

Soon it will be Easter and Avó gets ready for the special family gathering. She instructs her eldest son to buy special Easter gifts for the girls. She stuffs chocolate eggs inside gift bags and fluffs them up with reams of decorated paper.

"Do you know where Easter dinner will be this year? Is your brother hosting or will it be at his mother-in-law's?" Every day she asks her eldest son for news but he doesn't know anything about the plans. Until one night, close to the holiday, she manages to get a hold of her youngest son only to find out that he and his family are planning to be away at Easter; it's such a nice time to get away and he and his wife have been working so hard and could use some time to relax. "Sorry, Mãe."

"That's okay," she tells him. "As long as everybody's healthy, that's what I want for you."

On Easter morning, the kind lady takes her to church then drops her off at home. She wishes Avó a happy Easter with her family once they arrive later in the afternoon; that's what Avó has led her to think anyway. Then she locks the front door, puts her Sunday clothes away, prepares her lunch and eats while she watches the Portuguese news on television. Later she dozes off for just a bit, in between praying her rosary, the beads slipping from her fingers.

"António, why did you leave?" she complains to the photograph of her husband, younger and smiling, his arm around her on some Sunday afternoon as they strolled along the *Avenida* in Ponta Delgada. Then she watches another show; the voices from the television break the silence around her. It's still early evening but for tonight she decides to go to bed early.

"I'm tired," she convinces herself. "I hope my *queridas netas* are having a good vacation. As long as they're happy, I'm happy." Soon the spring will turn into summer, and then school will be out.

"I know I'll see them then."

RICHARD SIMAS

In Walls

Note #1. June 7, 2005. (Location: Front room (Deidre's), south wall, twelve feet from the adjoining wall facing the street. Pinned to the two-by-four stud spacer.)

When you know something of the past, you know something of the future. To whoever finds this, let me explain: we are the Sampsons, Don and Elizabeth, two children, Blaire and Deidre. We are renovating our home because we are cramped. I have decided to hide these notes in the walls, ceiling, and floors. It's a kind of game. I hope someday someone will read this and think for a moment about the lives of the people who lived here before. Maybe this note will never be found. I hadn't really thought of that. Keep looking. There are four more.

Dust.   Facing the wall with a sledgehammer, I raised the heavy tool, breathed once, and struck. A fist-sized hole was my brutal mark of begin-ning. I pounded repeatedly, but after a day and a half of stripping plaster from the front room and the hall ceiling, I needed help fast. You can't save money or time in renovations because it's never the way it looks in a power tool ad.

My hands were chafed raw, blistered, and too painful to tighten into a fist. I couldn't even sock myself. My fingers wouldn't uncurl while soaking them in the bathroom sink with ice cubes. Dust in my lungs provoked coughing fits at 2 a.m., waking my wife Elizabeth who fled to camp with the kids in the room off the kitchen. Hacking, and alone, I swore renovating was worth it.

"Call for help tomorrow morning," Liz had instructed firmly while sweep-ing dust. I couldn't grip the broom handle. "Show me your hands." She snapped a close-up of the swollen flesh. "I told you it was too much, but you don't listen." I do listen. She wished the project were finished rather than just starting. "What's your timeline on this again, John Optimist? A month? Did the engineer swear our building is on solid foundations?"

"Two weeks, ultimate max. Liz, the report cost us four hundred and fifty dollars. It says we're built on bedrock and the footings are solid. If it's a lie, we'll sue. You saw the report. We should be so stable at age eighty. Trust me, I don't take those kinds of risks." Liz scanned me in her ultrasound way.

A strip of skin had torn from the inside pad of my left thumb when it caught on a protruding, headless nail and dug a nasty gash. Bloodshed number two. I knew I should get a tetanus shot. I shifted in our bed, failing to protect the injury. The very moment my exposed flesh grazed the warm sheets Liz vacated, I opened my mouth to scream, pain jetting from thumb to shoulder. *Do it*, whispered the voice deep inside. That same instant, I conceived hiding five notes in the walls, ceiling, and floors of our renovation, just a few thoughts and facts, small intimate histories of our house and us. Nothing earth shattering, but it was my creativity, not a cute suggestion copied from a home decor magazine. I swear I listen to what is said to me. Was my cut already infected?

Next morning, I called Gino and Norman, two guys with a truck who charged thirty-five dollars an hour, hauling included. Their homemade advertisement taped to the wall in the convenience store two blocks from where we lived was a sign from the gods. My aching hand held the receiver. Gino's mom answered and searched for a pencil to note my name and number.

"No worry," she squeaked. "The boyz'll take care allathings." I feared they wouldn't show, but whenever you think for sure you're right, you're wrong. By three that afternoon, Gino and Norman had removed all the plaster and lath, yanked the nails from the studs, swept floors, and loaded rubbish. They were masters and gentlemen if not monks disguised as clean-up guys. I gave them a ten-dollar tip, said, *Thank you, thank you, thank you*, bowed and opened the front door for their exit. They sat in the truck smoking and listening to the radio, proof that not everyone is in a hurry and time is not always money. From their truck cab drifted a country ballad while two curly heads of hair kept beat. Demolition was done. A sweet and lonesome cowboy song clung to Saturday afternoon, wandering towards five p.m. Ohmmm.

I dialed my contractor and gave orders. "Hey Al, let's get going with those new walls on Monday." Upbeat, I stood center stage in the barren shell of the front room, legs wide, arms crossed in a man's stance, feeling like the ace of spades. I rode a single sheet of four by eight plywood that covered part of the floor joists so you wouldn't fall into the basement. Awaiting Al, I gazed through stripped studs into the next room and what used to be the entry wall. I peeked into the exposed ceiling joists where our renter-neighbor's clumsy feet were disturbingly closer to my head. Then from my plywood raft I searched the obscure underworld foundations of my home, pondering what to say in the notes.

"Right on, Don," Al jabbered. "Monday it is." Two live electrical wires dangled from a beam, their skinned, un-taped copper tips pointing at me.

"We'll start on your palace," Al added, unexpectedly whimsical.

My palace. My castle. Our home. Notes slipped under pink insulation pads or behind a stud before the drywall was screwed tight, jointed, and sealed. I saw my little speeches hidden for years in the dark caches. I wouldn't tell anyone because I'm afraid of not making sense to people, particularly my family. I would need a guide to remember which note was where. Jesus, I love to make lists.

"Great, great, great," I told Al, our palace contractor. I leaned on the stripped door casing in a casual, statue-king pose. Gino and Norman were returning to the monastery or rescuing someone else. God bless them, their secretary-mom, and the bulletin board where they advertise.

History. Smells released by demolition: dust, dry cedar splinters, horsehair insulation caulking the cracks, plaster, and rusty square-headed nails. The ordinary air of eighty-odd years of this and that: 1923–2005. Lives, seasons, hours, good and bad weather. Georges, Margarets, Franks, Lindas, and an ark-load of pets. An ice storm, seasonal blizzards, heat waves, and power outages. A Betty and a Mike whose mail still arrived occasionally. Sweat, tears, lemonade, gin and tea, the irrigation of time and dreams.

Then us: Liz, Don and kids Blair and Deidre. Unborn Anne, our three-month sleeping beauty embryo lost just after we moved in. I still name Anne as one in our nest, though miscarried from Liz's womb. Always. Liz didn't really recover until Deidre was born, and we all began living again.

Holidays, workdays, school days. Dumb and lost days; the forgotten, heroic, blank, and happy days. Angry, ecstatic, ordinary days. Kids' first school days and Halloween. Our house a dwelling, a sacred box, a cupboard, case, chest, closet, nook, and corner. Glory be to twelve years, 7139 Waverly Street is us and we are it. Amen.

Notary Bill Johnson handed Liz and me six decades of deeds and titles in a brown envelope when the deal was done, the history of previous owners. We signed our legal acts and sent them to city hall for registry, a gesture more solemn than our wedding. The house belonged to the bank and us, coupled in mortgage. The seller, a certain widow named Jenny Souza, out of the country and thus signing by proxy, was several hundred thousand dollars richer. Nice to meet you too, Jenny.

"This is your property's definitive history," notary Johnson rasped, a sage in a blue herringbone suit with tiny grey pinstripes, uttering words he shaved from sturdy, rough planks. "Store it in a secure and fire-proof place." I pushed his fat check for services rendered across the immense mahogany desk. The aged notary's deft right hand ventured out to fetch it.

The bank would visit our account every month for the next twenty-five years and subtract seven hundred and sixty-seven dollars in principal and interest. I figured we would acquire three square feet per thirty days. Terms negotiable in seven years. The brown envelope stuffed with legal details, a sacred text in the notary's eyes, was tossed on a pile of paper archives in the pantry next to the carton of coarse salt, and above a baseboard heater, conceivably the most combustible spot in the house. Many times I begged Liz to find a safer place for it. Filing is her job because her mind is much more orderly than mine.

I swung and struck with the sledgehammer, over and over, fracturing the wall, scattering plaster chips into the hall. Yes, I was demolishing part of our home with thirteen and a half years remaining on the mortgage, oh lucky numbers! It made me, yes, anxious. Friends told us renovation horror stories as if distributing homeopathic antidotes. No, I don't want to say I'm sorry yet, or that I have regrets.

Better.   Our plan was the same one many have once they believe their life is in control: make our home larger, more comfortable, and attractive. "The future, the kids," I told Liz. I was woozy from chamomile tea at 10 p.m. "They will grow and have parties and collections! Think of the future of your consulting business!" I yawned, pronouncing "future" like "urya." More space and light was the irresistible riff Liz and I chanted together. Eventually, we hoped for a deck to sit out in the sun.

We occupied the street level and basement of a two-story duplex in the Mile End of Montréal. Our renter lived in the apartment overhead, and we needed the revenue to make mortgage payments. Impossible to expand up or outwards, we would find space within, grabbing bits of lost or badly organized square footage. Mission possible: squeeze more from what we had, guide southern light to the very center of our abode, and live forever.

Optimizing space in our unfinished basement was an obvious first step, but reclaiming a portion of the hall and combining it with the living room at the front of the house was the brilliant coup that would create a surprising illusion of grandeur and transformation. An elegant salon was imaginable in the heart of our modest residence. Blinking into shafts of winter clarity in the dark months, we would marvel as it bounded through the house: spry, gracious, and youthful.

"Careful and tasteful positioning," chanted Fréderic, our architect. A gay Hercules with cutting-edge software, he shifted walls by sliding a tiny arrow with his little finger. *Click.* He removed the roof and second floor and offered us a bird's-eye view of our home. *Click and slide. Save.* He stood us in the hall-way to see how it might look walking through our virtual renovation to cello and saxophone accompaniment. *View.* Hand in hand, Liz and I ambled on screen. My jaw dropped. I pinched my forearm. I'm just a high school his-tory teacher, all grades, all eras. Fine with me.

"Prefer jazz? Shall I toss in some furniture just so you can imagine?" Fréderic coaxed devilishly yet distant enough. Classy Fred.

"Sure," said Liz.

"Don't bother," I answered, disturbed about how chic I looked on screen.

Blood was required, and sacrifice, two things I knew intimately and considered my specialty. Don't get me started. We opened a credit margin for cash against our twelve-year equity. Elizabeth and I gave up our shared office, formerly located in the front room. Early one Saturday morning, we crammed our files into the pantry behind the kitchen that had become tem-porary home archive headquarters. Bank statements and the kids' report cards were shelved next to the pasta, pancake mix, and canned goods just above the vacuum. I ate inexpensive but nutritious sardine sandwiches for lunch. We skimped on nearly everything, but it would be worth it.

Deidre would get the renovated front room, returning to where she was born eleven years previous on a marathon, freezing-rain Tuesday afternoon in March. Her birth was inscribed on those walls that I destroyed with the sledgehammer, a signature just as powerful as my own bashing. The scene was forever present in the room, stripped now to bare bones: Joan the midwife, Liz, and me, five hours of labor, a primal event shot with magic. I was terrified of losing another life, but Deidre emerged into the very air we breathed. Liz was a fury capable of destroying our house, such was her force in birthing, pushing on doorframes, and groaning like a storm. Deidre: purple and moist as a steamed plum, unfolded, screamed hello, and hasn't quieted since. Slimy and Buddha-faced, she fit exquisitely into my debutant father hands. We all wept and grabbed each other as if we'd just been saved from the end of the world. That all occurred in this room and Gino and Norman had just trucked away the plaster and rubbish remnants. Liz took a series of eerie, zebra-striped photographs of the walls with daylight cracking through the slanted lath.

Two feet in width gained by shifting the entry partition would make a grand room for Madam D. "Dad, can I have recessed lighting with a dimmer control?" Well, okay. She pleaded as only a female walking tightrope from childhood to adolescence could. "And crème walls with a pale Linden-green trim? Please no pink! I hate sissy crap." Where did she learn about recessed lighting and sissy crap?

Space needed. Attendance was increasing for Blaire's dining room trumpet concerts that made Zoom, our gimpy Calico cat, hide behind a door. Deidre was growing a woman's body and would need closets for her accoutrements. Liz did business on the kitchen counter and that couldn't continue for long. My needs? More hours in each day, infinite patience, and general perfecting, improvements that home renovation could never produce. Our nest risked implosion. I know, in other countries dozens live in smaller spaces, but that's not us. Deep in my chest the sounds "Provide, provide," chirped. I glided, searched, and figured, as a responsible bird must do. I found Al the contractor. We met with Fréderic. I summoned G & N. I imagined us perfect. I wanted the renovations right and craved a heroic moment. Just once. So why was hiding notes such a crazy idea? It was necessity, not a lark. Why a secret? One day, under the house's layer of skin, I would tell our story.

Note #2. June 8, 2005. (Location: pinned to the center-floor joist in the hallway, seven feet from the front door.)

Who lives here now? What is your life like? Is it you Deidre or Blaire, with your own family, renovating the way we did in 2005? What year is it? Am I still alive? How much does a litre of milk cost? A loaf of bread? Is the park still at the end of the street two blocks away or is everything different? I am curious about the house now and why you have discovered this note. If only I could know. I hope nothing horrible has happened and it has not been found in a pile of ruins full of dead bodies. Don.

Blood. It was first drawn when I sliced myself on the measuring-tape blade months before work began, a stain at the eighty-three inches mark. I was kneeling on the floor making rough sketches before the era of Fréderic, the iBook architect. Three thick dots of type O positive appeared on the wall in a dark, crimson smear. I wiped my index finger on my pants then inserted the injured flesh into my mouth as men in my family have always done. From that moment on, I couldn't walk that hallway without my eyes riveting on the bloodstain.

Beware of folly and impulse, the renovation oracles warned. Too late. In my mind, the notes had already hatched. Did I already say I am a stubborn man? I wanted them to be like a chain of clues, relating one to the other, perhaps the only way I know how to say anything. Like a family. Like the history I teach to distracted teens. We are never completely alone. It was not abstract art to say that life had inserted us into those walls, into the ceiling, and into the tongue-and-groove maple floor. It was mere fact and observation, and I was the simple secretary taking notes, praying that someone someday would come and hear me.

We are sorely lacking in history. I announced this at the dinner table the day before swinging the sledgehammer. We had obtained our permit from the city that morning, and I waved it in the air as if it was the Magna Carta. Blaire looked at me and frowned with his mouth full. There goes history-Dad again. He is a finely distilled version of my own screwed-tight sarcasm. A few nights later, after G & N had saved my botched demolition, thumb throbbing and wanting to celebrate Liz's return to our bed, I repeated my declaration for her benefit. "We are sorely lacking in history."

"Did you hurt yourself, Don?"

I was aching to tell her about the notes. She reached over, eyes still on her book, to touch my shoulder as only she does. My thumb pulsed as if a blood bank was collecting there. I should have known then it was infected.

"Phooey," Liz exclaimed. Odd things seduce me. "History. That's all people do these days is archive themselves as if every burp and fart is monumental. It's hysterical. Memory is just another muscle like your trapezoids or metatarsus, not some treasure chest." Devastating Liz. She was the ultimate resistance fighter of trivial emotion. You knew right away she didn't look through the same angled lens as everyone else. "History means zilch nowadays. Time is now. Nothing is past." A natural performer, she could cant like a pop analyst or a clairvoyant at the drop of a coin, impeccable tone and rhythm, winning her moment every time. No surprise she is deft in business.

"Interesting," I said.

"Look. What you can't remember, you probably don't need," she argued. "Engrave that on my tombstone, okay?" I had imagined her ashes in a transparent Mason jar labeled, "Voilà Liz, Savante." She is no fool and recites history as if Herodotus had been reincarnated as a post-modern, forty-one-year-old hipster. She plays her joker cards with icy assurance.

"But Liz, without history we are nothing," I protested, squirming closer under the sheets.

"Horse crap. That would be delightful," she snipped. "We are mostly water anyway, much of it murky. You're dead wrong." My Liz: prickly buds of cool commentary and intolerance for ambivalence.

"Just wrong is fine, thanks," I answered. Compromise and a truce were in order. I knew the battlegrounds and didn't want her warm body escaping me again. Our exchange made me tumble more deeply in love with her, with the notes I would write, with the whole dusty ordeal of renovation, and the missed measures of life in general. I was destined for such affections. She yawned massively the way sleepy lions might after digesting the necks of baby gazelles. I rubbed my left eye until it stung and was glad my right hand was healthy in case her body desired care later.

"What's most important to you anyway?" Her query caught me off guard, coupled as it was with suddenly extinguishing the reading light. Her book hit the floor in the dark. She swallowed two aspirins and a gulp of water then crossed her arms. Why with lights out, I'll never understand. I sincerely wanted to respond, but I am slow and cautious in the dark, especially when tightly woven wild animal nets dangle above my head. Our room's obscurity swelled to engulf us. I had renovations to figure, five notes to write and hide, and the mysteries of sleep to encounter.

"Think Gino and Norman paint too?" I whispered a few minutes later, just as they entered my dreams with their shovels. Thirty-five dollars an hour, hauling included; that's what's important to me.

After sleep-hour one, I found myself suddenly standing in that demolished front room, naked except for a pair of thin blue cotton boxers hugging my waist. I wasn't conscious of how I got there, but there aren't forty possibilities. The injured thumb throbbed painfully, and that's when the third note came to me in a complete and final draft. Not a word was changed after I wrote it on one side of letter-sized white paper. But before signing my name, something happened.

When I was a child, I thought that all cellars and basements were hells teeming with snakes, poison, and demons. We were Catholics with firm beliefs and vivid imaginations where work was Purgatory and Paradise a day off at the beach. I pressed my pen to the paper, writing Note #3, kneeling on the sheet of plywood that covered the floor joists and kept me from falling into hell. The musty odor of snakes, poison, God's wrath, and demons rose from below, and I realized that only three-quarters of an inch of construction material separated us.

Note #3. June 9, 2005. (Location: under the new birch floor, absolute center in Deidre's 'crème and linden' room.)

Here is our house's legal history, sixty years of records, indicating dates, names and prices each time the property has changed hands. These are hard facts, and I think it's important to have them correct on paper. Look how the value grew, the names of the owners and all the fancy legal language: Anatole, Bertrand, Maximillian Dunberry, like kings and counts. Whoever reads this, I hope you will look around and imagine the history here, even if it all sounds a bit strange . . .

She entered the room silently and embarked on the sheet of plywood. Occasionally, she floats rather than walks. I heard the slow shutter click of her Nikon. She came upon me like wind to a sail, warm and moist, her salty mouth drinking the back of my neck. Murmuring. Hands encircled me and probed my chest, weight pressing into me. Imprisoned, my sole desire was eternal condemnation. Bind and blindfold me sweet gale. Ravish me. On that four-by-eight piece of plywood shifting and tipping under us in the demolished room, on a splendid sea, our bodies tossed and exploded. "What are you up to?" She asked. "What's on that paper?" I answered with a primitive sound. Smeared with blood from where I snagged my skin, Note #3 slipped from my hand and fell into the basement where I would retrieve it later from hell with a flashlight and hide it safely.

"If your marriage survives renovations, it can endure anything," experienced friends projected. Work progressed. My infected finger swelled. Regardless of our constant precautions, dust drifted throughout the house. I hung plastic tarps, taped edges, sealed cracks, swept, and vacuumed. We closed the doors to other rooms but during the weeks of work, a fine residue still found its way into the kitchen drawers, under the toilette seat, into our clothes, the butter dish. Impossible places. It clung to our soles and left a powdery trail wherever we walked.

Liz photographed dust on the windowpanes, bent nails, and doors removed from their hinges. She shot packs of new materials as they arrived, Al smoking a cigarette, and his carpenter calculations penciled onto studs. Her eyes searched and exposed our home in the unexpected moments. My project was to hide us in the walls; hers would bare us naked.

Guilt Forgiveness.

> **Note #4.** June 11, 2005. (Location: the inside wall, new living room, four feet from the floor, taped to the wiring.)

> *My son Blaire wrote these words in indelible black felt marker when renovations were almost finished. He listens to old blues songs and this one must have special meaning for him. The lyrics are permanently inscribed all over the new wall. I have no idea what kind of man he will be.*

> *Baby, let me follow you down*
> *Baby, let me follow you down*
> *Well I'd give anything in this God-almighty world*
> *if you just let me follow you down.*

"Damn it, you erase that, Blaire," I said. He refused and locked himself in his room. I exploded, pounding on his door, but he pushed the bed up against it. I swore again.

"Go away, go away idiot," he said. I was ready to tear the house apart. Sometimes we aren't who we think we are. When Blaire was two I spanked him hard undeservedly and still regret it. When I pleaded for forgiveness, he gave me a look of bewilderment and fear that I will never forget.

"You don't care about everything we've done," I yelled.

"The house was better before the stupid renovations," he screamed back. "It was a ridiculous idea and a waste of money."

"Cool off," Liz grumbled, "the damned paint will cover it." I heard ghosts singing *Baby, let me follow you down*, throughout the house. Blaire was brasher than me, ranting right on the living room wall where everyone could hear instead of whispering in a hidden place. Calm Liz stopped talking and Deidre sang nursery rhymes she had abandoned years earlier. I couldn't lift my arm to pound Blaire's door. I called Al.

"Let's get this finished fast," I begged.

Our house was out of hand and we were caught in its disorder. You read about a maniac burying a dozen people in the backyard after hacking the bodies into bits. You hear about average folks suddenly losing control, or about something minor that starts a raging fire. That wasn't going to happen, but somber thoughts occurred to me when time came for the last note. I would write the ugly parts too, the pain, failure, and our loneliness, and hide it in a safe, secretive place, a key to understanding the other notes. I needed to hurry because Al was closing the last section of wall.

I knew what to say, but I couldn't lift my arm to write. The infection had spread, aching up into my shoulder and neck. My skin was pale, the corners of my eyes glazed and yellow when I looked in a mirror. I took a cab to emergency and called Liz at work. During the three days in the hospital she took charge, marshalling renovations to an end. Deidre and Blaire helped out and visited me with flowers and get well soon cards. According to the doctor, I barely avoided amputation. One-armed renovation heroes are rare.

As I approached our door the night I returned home from the hospital, a brisk wind was tempting the treetops, and I was relieved to enter and smell fresh paint. The kids were asleep. Furniture remained piled in the renovated salon and dining room in what looked like someone else's home. Liz caught me in the hall and took me in her arms. She climbed up on my feet where I ferried her to the kitchen and she poured us red wine. "You okay?"

I was weary, but instead of resting I wandered around admiring the house's dimmed, recessed-lighting elegance. Our walls were straight. Al had varnished the new, yellow birch floor to a stunning luster. The doors fit snugly in their casings for the first time ever. In her new room, Deidre shifted in crème and linden shadows when I gave her a goodnight kiss. She was arguing with someone in a dream. I tacked a sheet across the curtain-less window to block the orange streetlight nipping her feet.

Into the renovated dining room painted in desert hues I roamed. Fred was a genius. We lived in a palace. The new wall where Blaire's blues lyrics had been written was the color of reptiles near Santa Fe. With my still sensitive thumb I traced his words on the desert wall. *Baby, let me follow you down,* I repeated, hoping they would remain. Liz chanted a new language in her sleep that I would have to learn. The whole house was speaking except for me. I remembered the unwritten Note #5.

> *What will be left of us in the end? Handfuls of dust? Sand words escaping your hands? A wall chanting to you when you stand with the sledgehammer to destroy it? These are our imperfect lives. Don, Liz, Deidre, Blaire, and (Anne).*

I raised my fist to strike. April wind snapped at the house, and I preferred to be within. Our house shuddered with pleasure and pain, trembling on its foundations and the bedrock they anchored in. The expert engineer was wrong after all, and I have already forgotten where I hid the notes.

EDITH BAGUINHO

Eternity, Cuts In/

1.   (2:11)

hunting for living food sources, hieroglyphics/ Ferreira or Smith, your
name is your trademark/ illiteracy, picture shingle/ the self-employed, busi-
ness cards / the birth of a need, a free product sample/ fresh produce, the
open farmers' market/ common sense housewares, your freeway Ikea store/
a fiery sun blazing into the Atlantic, an Expedia billboard across silver skies
promoting vacations to Cuba in January/ vandalism, wall graffiti/ a starry
starry night, store window mannequins wearing Prada and sporting Gucci
bags/ walking beneath a street-corner lamp dressed to kill, silent, the oldest
profession in the world/a close-up of a human female eye, CoverGirl® mas-
cara/ dull knives, town crier/ repeated www.visits, Metamucil spam/ scoop
the dog poop, a Milk initiative/ biggest spending advertisers, government
politicians/ used gold shops abound, sidewalk easel signage/

2.   (1:46)

an infant's laughter, Toys "R" Us commercials right before Christmas time/
the sacrament of Baptism, a church pulpit/ Hallowe'en, store sale signs out
with witches and ghosts/ Christmas, Santa Claus parade letters /child-
hood, McDonald's—the Cracker Jack substitute/ adolescence, propaganda
extravaganza and a parent's nightmare/ aches and pains, your friendly
street-corner drugstore/ civility, street sidewalk cafés/ socializing, sharing a
Coors Light Special/ reading famous authors, Penguin Classics/ and not-
so-famous ones, word-of-mouth small presses/ cigarette butts, a native per-
son's vengeance on sidewalks/ Perrier water, Summerlicious dining deals/

substance abuse, Franciscan programmes proclaiming good news/ aging, pharmaceutical company badgering/

3. (2:01)

the centre of human history, a Saviour is born to us/ the Holy Grail, a fast food counter/ portable rainy day domes, Knirps umbrellas at a store entrance/ cleanliness, soap and water/ a cold and snowy night, hot cocoa vending machines/ self-worth, a New Age heresy/ feel-good optimism, positive energy babble via stones/ natural disasters, World Relief Organizations/ free will concept, the Bible/ waking up, a Turkish coffee delight/ falling asleep, herbal tea opium from the Far East/ fidelity, the marriage sacrament / grocery shopping, brands and No Name brand/ a dewy field of lavender in Tipperary, a floating RE/MAX hot air balloon/ honey bees buzzing around flowers, Bee Maid honey/ fields of grain, multi-grain bread/ an open bottle of fine Port wine, a Sandeman label/ paradise lost, the power of prayer/

4. (4:07)

entering a highway, BMW billboard/ a socialite, Cartier magazine advertisement/ an antiquarian, first editions only/ proletarian unrest, protest signs and marches/ algebra and mathematics, barons banking billions/ Alexandria's legacy, visit your local library/ a museum, house of muses/

artifact collections, what's-his-name—the collector/ the heart of darkness' memorial grave, US manifest destiny/ cars, oil-run conglomerates/ rivals, air-powered and solar-powered technologies/ meeting famous people, the autograph/ the *Mamma Mia* musical, the film, then DVD hype/ a city's downtown core, signs covering automobiles, buses, and buildings/ free parking spot, human billboard/ Cohen's *Hallelujah* playing on the radio, a Billboard magazine/ the Iraqi war and all wars before and after it, newspaper stands everywhere/ *Wheel of Fortune*, a Procter & Gamble TV commercial/ followed by *Jeopardy*, a Procter & Gamble TV commercial/ sports games live, captive stadium audiences/ the Super Bowl, a Christian anti-abortion commercial/ this commercial's aftermath, media network analyst gurus' anti-last words/ the Rock of Gibraltar, a travel agent's business card/ the song *Just Beat It*, a music video/ *Carmen*—the opera, a programme's du Maurier display advertisement/ a night out at the movies, Coke commercials with a family of bears/ the Tango, *Dancing with the Stars*/ slavery, "I am a victim" mantra/programme cuts, Nielsen's low ratings/ the poor, "Always with us" prophecy/ pollution, Go Green government incentives/ the interjection "¡Olé!," bullfight poster/ T-shirts with legible writing, a walking message board/ knowledge, monopoly-run media/ a new idea, only a jingle, jangle away/

5.   (00:24)

the explosion of a new day, door-to-door flyers/ the Incarnation, St. Gabriel's visit/ to end all of this, highlight then press the delete key/ to make it last forever, just save/

ALGARVE, APRIL 2011

ESMERALDA CABRAL

Three Candles for the Virgin Mary

The cobblestones of my youth crumble beneath my feet. I put on miles every day walking the streets of Lisbon, climbing hills, dodging cars and colliding into puffs of cigarette smoke exhaled by restaurant waiters who lean against buildings while on their coffee break. It's my first time in Lisbon since all the loss—since my mother, father and sister died, one after another, three deaths in four years. It is strange to be here without them because Lisbon was our city. When we lived in São Miguel in the Azores over nine hundred miles away, and even after we moved to Canada, Lisbon was our destination of choice for family holidays.

I've avoided coming here since they left me. I was afraid of the sadness I'd feel confronting so many memories. But now, the time feels right. I'm here at a writing conference and I plan to carve time from the full days to remember my darling ones, to reflect on how different my life is now without them, and to write. It is my hope that being back in Lisbon, and writing, will help bring order to the chaos of my grief.

I should be looking up to see the beauty of the city, but my gaze is pulled to the ground and the uneven maze of stones with its mesmerizing patterns. There are holes here and there, worn cobblestones that have been picked out and will be replaced later; others are still there but they're loose and they move when I step on them. The pattern is disrupted but there is beauty, despite the brokenness, and I can't help but look down.

I turn a corner near the pastry shop in the city centre and I can almost feel my sister Maria's presence. We sat here so many times, in the sun, to sip on a cool drink and feast on pastries. I think of her smile, exposing a neat row of even, white teeth, and how she would throw her head back in delight when she laughed.

Several men are working on the cobblestones near the stairs to the subway station. One man loosens and lifts the stones, one at a time, with a large pick while others rearrange and set stones in newly-laid cement, re-establishing the pattern. The men's bare sweaty backs glisten in the sun.

I walk across Rossio, now the main square in downtown Lisbon, but once the site of public executions during the Inquisition. I decide to visit the nearby church, Igreja de São Domingos, where the sentences were read out and from which the prisoners would begin their death march to the square. The columns of stone in this building date back to 1241 and the church miraculously survived two massive earthquakes, and more recently, a fire in the 1950s.

Inside, I'm struck by the smell of smoke and the charred pillars that remain. It's as if both are lingering witnesses to the events of the past. The first time I visited this church I was ten years old. The dark, gloomy interior scared me, as did the dilapidated statues of the saints. I could swear they were all looking at me. My mother, my sister Maria and I had come to Lisbon to visit my eldest sister, Toni, who was still at university and had not immigrated with us to Canada.

I have a vivid image of Maria on that trip. She was a beautiful, confident twenty-year-old, and she manoeuvred the cobblestones so well in her platform shoes. She wore big sunglasses, yellow plaid palazzo pants and a black blazer; her hair flew back in the wind and people stared at her. I watched her with little sister awe and wondered if I could ever look like her when I grew up.

We had walked around the perimeter of the pews like the other tourists to look at the statues of the saints, each with a row or two of candles at the base. We passed the statue of the Virgin Mary and my mother stopped and crossed herself. *In the name of the Father, and of the Son, and of the Holy Spirit.* She lit a candle at the base of the statue of Mary, and gave me a coin to drop into the little box. Klunk. The coin made a hollow sound; there weren't many others in there. My mother knelt on the padded step and removed a rosary from her purse. I waited impatiently as my sister Maria walked to the next statue, and then the next. The statue of Mary was in perfect condition. Unlike some of the other statues, there weren't any chips of plaster missing and her face had been carefully painted. Mary had a faint smile and I thought she was looking down, right at my mother.

"*Mamã*, what are you doing?" I asked. I shifted my weight from one leg to another, and wondered how long we'd be stopped here.

"Praying to Mary. I'm asking her to protect you girls," she said. "I won't be long."

I remember thinking hard, trying to come up with a good reason to light a candle too. But I had no special requests back then.

I followed Maria to the back of the church and then out to the vestibule where we waited for our mother. There were two beggars, a man and a woman, sitting on either side of the stone steps, asking visitors for money. Most people ignored them but some stopped to drop coins into their cups.

That evening, a bomb went off in the military quarter near Toni's apartment. It was February 1972, two years before the revolution that would overthrow the Salazar regime. Toni was late getting home that night and my mother was frantic. The power went out. I sat on the couch and cried as my sister and mother searched the cupboards and drawers for candles and matches. My mother lit several candles and set them on the window sills. She stared out the window. We could hear people yelling, whistles blowing and sirens in the distance. My mother began reciting the *Magnificat*, her prayer of choice when she was really scared. I'd heard her say this prayer many times, usually during thunderstorms or on plane trips.

Toni walked through the door an hour or so later. She'd been held up by a student protest but she was unharmed. My mother ran to hug her and thanked the Virgin Mary out loud. Maria brought out a pack of cards and we proceeded to play games by candlelight long into the night, grateful that we were all together, and safe.

I'm back in Lisbon, on my own now, and back in this church, nearly forty years after that first visit. I walk around the pews like the other tourists, and I look at the saints on the wall. They've been restored, I think, since I was here last. So much has happened in my life in the last few years that I still feel unsteady when I think about it. First, my mother died after being afflicted with dementia and then cancer. My father's death came nine months later from a fall and brain haemorrhage. And then, incredibly, we lost Maria, to cancer too. Toni and I scrambled to adjust to the inevitability of our sister's death but we didn't have much time: Maria died four months after she started to feel ill. I wanted so much to provide her with comfort and reassurance the way she would for me when I was feeling down or troubled but comfort eluded all of us then. The three of us would sit together, glass-beaded rosaries in hand, on Toni's overstuffed couch, and begin reciting the long string of Hail Marys. In my private moments, though, I resorted to the *Magnificat*.

I'm still trying to figure out how my prayers were answered. Maybe the miracle lies in that I feel no anger, just sadness, at Maria's death.

At the statue of Mary I kneel on the padded step to say a prayer. I'm not sure what to say. I study Mary's porcelain face, an oval of alabaster skin framed by a blue cloak covering her head and draping her shoulders. I sense kindness in her eyes and faint smile. "Oh, Mary, why did Maria have to die? I miss her so much."

I decide to light three candles. One for my mother, another for my father, and a larger one, a special one, for Maria. Today would have been her birthday.

I drop three coins into the box to the right of the statue. I take the match and light my candles, one by one. The tears well up in my eyes and I turn away and rush to the back of the church and out the door, desperate for sunshine and fresh air. My head whirls in the bright light and I reach out to steady myself against the cold stone of the pillar that frames the church's entrance. There's a woman sitting on the steps nearby. She is beautiful, with glossy black hair pulled back in a tight bun, sad green eyes, and skin made brown and lined by the sun. I've seen this woman on these steps before, begging, as church-goers and tourists stream into the church. She looks at me but doesn't say anything, doesn't ask for money. I start to walk away, still looking at her, and she gives me a faint smile.

"*Vá com Deus*," she says. Go with God.

PAUL SERRALHEIRO

Railroad Men

The tracks were fastened to the earth.
They hugged the sides of mountains and ran
the rims of lakes. Rain or shine we clattered out
to the machines on work cars in the morning
to pull rusted spikes, topple worn short rails
and lay quarter-mile ribbons of gleaming grey-blue metal.
The men were mute at work, their thick hands
hanging onto clanging machines
that blasted the countryside
and shoulder to shoulder we slammed
the stubborn ends of rails
all arms heaving to make them fit.

I had come for adventure, a dreamer kid
doing a tough man's work. But as I pulled gnarled spikes
from oiled cross-ties and tossed them into piles
on the rails' gravel bed,
I studied the rock faces of mountains
the streams that meandered through the woods
and the still pools I threw rocks into
the ripples widening like music or flights of birds.
And I listened to the men at rest, their tall talk
of women and brawls, and drank with them in town.

When I left to ride the train back home
at the end of May, the ravines and gullies
we rattled by were gorged with green
thick lush grass and bushes, droplets of rain hanging
like crystal bracelets from the fine wrists of trees.
I could feel every muscle and my hands were tougher.
I now knew iron and steel,
the rusted old and the new kind
in which you saw your reflection
if you looked hard enough.

The Return

the old women were at the nets
needling the ropework with gnarled fingers
the eyes of the men were cold
they muttered amongst themselves
huddled on the shore
their voices dulled with distance
as the sails became firm with a breeze
bellying breasts
with the water cutting under the keel
and i, jamming the tiller
went off over granite waters
till the day bled beautifully
whereupon i lowered the sails
and the hull plowed through sand
and i landed and had my fill of wine
and went down with the day
having sailed since noon

i was determined to sail alone
to live the solitude of the sea
having cursed the townspeople and the gods
but the wind turned round
when nights beyond a lantern's eye
the sea was swelling to a torment of tossing
and the ship was mad with rocking
charred clouds crowded from portside
and i pledged favours to the gods
to Poseidon and to Zeus

and then I cursed them bitterly
while a thousand fears tore me
and i wished that the tide
batter the ship to splinters against the cliffs

then the morning
i remember a mild breeze milking the sails
the water lapped moist against the hull
as i sailed away from the homeland
from the people and the gods

EDUARDO BETTENCOURT PINTO

Abril entre a chuva

Canta como a água a insubmissão e as torrentes.
Deixa entre as rochas que escurecem
na noite mais longa a vertigem
da tua passagem.
Sê o archote dentro dessa música, o pó e o sândalo
do grito.
Entre os dedos de um profeta descobre um voo de sinais.
Só então poderás
cobrir o mundo de sementes
na vastidão de outro poema.

April between rain

Sing like the rebellious water and its torrents.
Leave among the darkening rocks,
in the longest night, the vertigo
of your passage.
Be the torch within this music, the powder and sandalwood
its scream.
Discover a flight of signs between the fingers of a prophet.
Only then can you cover
the world of new beginnings
within the vastness of another poem.

Poema do litoral

São areia, brancos e leves,
teus pés miúdos.
Que rumor deixam?
Vens ainda de setembro, descalça,
o verão quase no fim.
Sobre ti cai
a inocente luz das palmeiras.
Gota a gota bebes
todo o oiro da tarde.
Que me dizes agora,
tão perto os meus olhos
da nuvem branca que atravessa
o céu e a memória?
A minha voz corre ao teu encontro
—nunca voou assim, tão alta
sobre o mundo.

Coastal poem

They are sand, your small feet,
white and light.
What murmur do they leave behind?
You're returning from September still, barefoot,
the summer almost over.
The innocent light of palm trees
falls upon you.
Drop by drop
you drink the gold of the afternoon.
What do you tell me now,
my eyes so close
to a white cloud passing through
the sky and memory?
My voice races towards you
    —never has it flown like this, so high
over the world.

Madrigal rente à primavera

Começo a ouvir o teu nome com o cantar das aves.
Chove na música das primeiras sílabas
e uma abelha voa entre o rumor dos teus cabelos.
Vens de muito longe, do momento em que uma pétala
se abriu sobre o esplendor do mundo.
Tão pura a água que corre entre o silêncio
e o deserto onde a manhã se enche de gritos!
Começo a ouvir-te como se numa terra em chamas
os meus passos fossem as ervas que um dia pisaste
enquanto dançavas de braços abertos
à minha solidão, infinita e glacial.

Madrigal near spring

I begin to hear your name with the birds singing.
It rains down in the music of the first syllables
and a bee flies within the murmur of your hair.
You come from far away, from the moment a petal
opened over the splendour of the world.
As pure as the water that flows between silence
and the desert where the morning fills with screams!
I begin to hear you as if on a land ablaze
as if my steps were the herbs you stepped on
while you danced with open arms
to my loneliness, endless and glacial.

Macau

Onde dorme o tempo nestas ruas estreitas?
Cobre-se de sombras naquela casa?
Será aquele velho de bengala
que pisa fatigado o chão de abril
e sobe as escadas gastas,
degrau a degrau?
Todo o seu corpo
corre a cor das buganvílias,
desenha na parede
um itinerário de água curvada.
Cercado pelos labirintos da idade,
o cansaço de ser homem
é mais antigo
que a cidade.

Macau

Where does time sleep in these narrow streets?
Is it covered by shadows in that house?
Could it be the tired old man with a cane
stepping down on April's ground
and climbing the worn stairs,
one by one?
His entire body
runs with the colour of the bougainvillea
and draws a curved path of water
upon the wall.
Surrounded by the labyrinths of age,
the weariness of being a man
is older
than the city.

TRANSLATIONS BY FERNANDA VIVEIROS,

WITH THE AUTHOR

ANTONIO M. MARQUES

The Last Shot

Since he had retired the year before, Fred Campos lived like a ghost. His steps would take him anywhere which was nowhere as soon as he got there. However, he was retired because he had wanted to and was not at all sorry for it. He had always been a bit of a thinker, and how that helped, with all the free time he had on his hands. His achievements in the field he had chosen, architecture, had been many and he had received kudos from both clients and employers over the years. At the beginning of his retirement he used to sometimes think about this or that project and how clearly he'd brought it to fruition. He thought he excelled at his work and the accolades only confirmed the idea he had of himself, that of being a thorough man with talent.

After a few months though, he began to be bothered by an indistinct uneasiness. Remembrances of past successes suddenly stopped having any effect on him and they began dissolving into themselves as into an ever contracting spiral, and with them vanished the source of his self-esteem. In hindsight it dawned on him that he had really accomplished nothing, or very little at best. What had he really done? Were his achievements mere trophies?

Soon after retiring, Campos had begun to spend some time, every day, at the club Hourbind, playing cards. But he could play only for so long. Now, he was restless. He couldn't stand the inanity of the game. It was a waste of time, a distancing from life, that's what it was. The club had been recommended to him by his son, Joachim, and most of the men there were all his own age or thereabouts, mostly retired people enjoying their supposedly halcyon days. Campos felt little congeniality in the place.

He would leave Hourbind when restlessness became unbearable and he'd roam the streets aimlessly. But the next day he'd be there again, his days repeating in the same pattern like a wheel in its axle. He realized the futility of his walks. No amount of walking calmed his agitation. What should he do? How should he change his situation? His strength, his orientation, his pragmatism, his very understanding of things was not the same as they were before he retired. And the more he thought, the more his brain ticked on, unable to crystallize a solution.

He could see that he lacked options now because he'd taken things for granted most of this life. He had followed, followed, followed, and he had accepted. And when he realized this, the distance of his walks increased. He went to Hourbind, but would leave soon after he got there.

"You should buy a car, Fred," one of his friends at the club told him.

"I like to walk," he replied drily.

He'd sold his car soon after retiring and all of his commuting was done either by bus or streetcar. And he liked walking because he could think more clearly. That was the important point. He loved the process of thinking. His thoughts were his best friends and his worst enemies. He loved them, because they gave him this sense of freedom, of lucidity; but at the same time, his thoughts brought him disquiet. He couldn't find peace as things stood. He didn't want to accept them. He'd had enough of acceptance. He had to leave his mark, show his dissatisfaction with the situation that surrounded him.

Most of the stories Fred heard at Hourbind were stories of despair and sorrow. They didn't help his mood. Once in a while someone boasted about a grandson or granddaughter, but Fred rarely lent a kind ear to these tales. He refused to spend an hour out-swaggering the other fellow on account of his grandchildren. He wouldn't share vicarious optimism. Stories of misery, though, were an everyday affair, and they were repeated ad nauseam.

Fresh stories were added to everyone's repertoires and were dissected with animation.

There was, for instance, the case of Roy Lato's neighbour. The neighbour's son had been killed, shot in the head, while peddling drugs. The news lasted nearly two weeks with all the seniors arguing in a cacophony of voices, discussing not only the problem of the drugs but the steps that led a young man to take and abuse them. There was nothing innovative in their way of thinking and yet it was something which kept them somewhat alert.

The drug killing was eventually supplanted by Jovial Tom's crisis. He had been unemployed for over a year and was applying for welfare although he was only fifty and by no means an invalid. In fact, Jovial Tom had been known to brag about his health and strength and boasted of being able to outperform men half his age. Yet he had no place to use his abilities after his company downsized and laid him off. At his age, jobs didn't grow on trees, as he himself had put it. This forced paralysis stopped the flow of money and he'd begun to use his own savings to boost his wife's low wages as a cook's assistant. He was nervous and despondent, even snappy at times.

"It would be all right if I didn't have a twenty-eight-year-old handicapped daughter," he explained, his eyes darting about for a sign of encouragement from the old men at Hourbind. "I want to make sure she's taken care of before I die."

Jovial Tom knew his savings would soon run out and his daughter, Angelica, would be left with nothing. Once he and his wife were gone, she would have to rely on luck and on other people's generosity. He knew of institutions that could look after her, institutions that wouldn't charge payments "but what kind of care would she get in a place like that," he asked out loud, "without her having some money of her own?" He was not a very optimistic fellow.

"Miseries, miseries, miseries," Fred Campos muttered as he walked out of the club and took refuge in his reveries.

Fred saw his son once a month. He'd go to Joachim's home, have a meal and spend a few hours playing with his grandsons. His daughter-in-law, Lavinia, was a kind woman who always received him warmly. Independent professionals, his son was a professor at the university while Lavinia worked as an editor in a publishing house specializing in pulp fiction. There was no lack of money in that family. His son asked him to come and see them more often, to eat with them and play with the kids but he wouldn't go. Once a month was enough. Better wanted than . . .

A day came when he couldn't stand the atmosphere in the club and walked out after having listened yet again to Jovial Tom's story about Angelica and her sad future. This bit of news was already on its third week and showed no sign of slowing. On the day Fred walked out, he had planned to visit his son. He had phoned the day before to announce his visit but now he wished he hadn't called. He'd rather be alone to think his thoughts out as he sensed there was something struggling within him that wanted to get said. The restlessness he usually felt was even more acute today and he felt like erupting. He had no wish to exchange banalities with either his son or daughter-in-law much as he loved them. He didn't want the germinating idea he could feel taking shape in his mind to die away. He wanted to be ready when it sprouted and make of it what he was supposed to. His talks with his son were not inspiring or conducive to bringing forth ideas. Their conversations were desultory, rumbling, their only connection being the underlying acceptance existing between them as a family. They spoke only on subjects they could agree on and avoided things on which they might disagree, such as, for instance, the politics of the working place or how governments were geared to dehumanize people.

They touched once or twice on these issues but soon realized they didn't share a common understanding of them. After all, they were of different generations and viewed life differently. Fred didn't really mind the lack of passion in their talks. As it stood, things ran smoothly between them and he wanted them to remain so. He remembered he'd had disagreements with his father, and that Joachim had had disagreements with him. He had told his father that he knew what he wanted to do with his life, and his own son had told him the same.

"Please, Lord, don't let me die a failure. Let me have a last shot at life," Fred prayed.

Fred Campos rang up his son and cancelled his visit. Yes, he'd go the next day. He roamed the streets for most of the night. He examined his life, his future. Thoughts came to him, and then fled. He let them go. His thoughts were still churning as he went to bed. It was only in the small hours of the morning that he finally fell asleep. He woke up late, around noon, exhausted. He usually got up before seven but today was different. His legs were weary and his feet sore from walking for so many hours. The poor night's sleep had left his mind numb but he had, nevertheless, reached a decision. He wondered how his son would take it.

As it turned out, his son wouldn't take it at all. Fred waved the children away after dinner. "You don't want to play with the kids, Dad?" "Later," he answered. The men sat down on the sofa with their coffees and Fred broached the subject that had kept him walking for so many hours. Joachim wouldn't hear of it. How could his father come out with such an outlandish proposition? There were institutions to take care of cases like that.

"This is unheard of." He was emphatic. "You have grandsons to think of, you know."

"They will be alright. They're healthy kids and they have you and Lavinia. You will give them a comfortable life, I'm sure."

"Only God knows the future. We don't. God helps those who help themselves."

"God, God, God. Everyone wants to cash in on his name." Fred sighed. "Joachim, I paid for your doctorate. You work only the hours you want, or nearly. You have money coming in from several sources. What do you want more money for?

"Still, it's my money, isn't it? I want it."

"No, it's my money."

At the door, with Lavinia looking on wide-eyed and puzzled, Joachim tried again.

"Pa, don't do anything rash. Don't do anything you may regret later."

Fred didn't answer.

"Pa, think of what Ma would say."

"Don't bring your mother into this. Let her rest in peace." Fred didn't want to think about his wife who'd died three years before he retired. They had talked often about travelling the world as soon as he retired but her unexpected death had ended that particular dream.

"Pa, if you go ahead with your mad idea, I'll have to take some drastic steps."

Fred descended the front stairs of his son's home without replying. The night air was nippy and he pulled his jacket tightly over his chest and neck. It was late October and the temperature fell quickly in the evenings. He hurried his steps a bit although his legs were still so tired. He shivered. My son threatened me. What kind of drastic steps will he take? Accuse me of senility, of dementia? It's what one generation uses against the older one. Let it be what it has to be. It wouldn't do to turn my back on a challenge this late in life. Things have to take their course. I'll start them rolling . . . with drastic steps of my own.

A month later he married Angelica.

LAUREANO SOARES

A Mala de Cartão

Parti um dia do meu berço natal,
da terra onde nasci
do meu Sobral,
com uma simples mala na mão.
Uma mala em cartão.
Contendo como riqueza
umas peças de roupa . . .
Sonhos!
algo risonhos
e muita ilusão.

Segui o meu caminho pela vida fora
vivi alegrias e tristezas sem fim
desses momentos
eu me lembro agora
das penas que feriram o meu coração
e dos meus olhos brotaram:
Pérolas cintilantes
que vieram quebrar-se
desfeitas no chão.

Da (pobre) riqueza que eu trouxe outrora
ficaram os sonhos e pouca ilusão.
Há desses momentos que a minha alma chora
quando me recordo da mala em cartão.

The Cardboard Suitcase

One day I left my homeland,
the place where I was born
my village of Sobral,
with only a suitcase in my hand.
A cardboard suitcase
whose only wealth
was a few pieces of clothing . . .
Dreams!
Cheerful ones
and lots of illusions.

I followed my path through life
in the world outside
living out endless joys and sadness
now I remember those moments
the sorrows that hurt my heart
and glittering pearls
that flowed from my eyes
shattering on
the ground below.

All that's left of the (poor) wealth I took with me
are dreams and a few illusions.
There are times when my soul weeps
as I think back on my cardboard suitcase.

A Voz do Poeta

Escutai, ó gentes a voz que canta,
Como a do rouxinol nos arvoredos.
Despertando a madrugada entre olmedos,
Saltando de ramo em ramo se espanta.

Ó guitarra minha, portuguesa, santa,
Ó poeta que vais versejando sem medo,
Trinando, por amor, na vida sem segredo
A tua poesia as águas do rio encanta!

Cessai rios cantantes de água pura,
Marulhando, descendo a rocha dura,
Escutai minha guitarra seleta.

A guitarra geme, a poesia reza;
Murmurando sonhos de grande beleza:
Tempos de paixão na vida do poeta.

The Poet's Voice

Listen, people, to the voice that sings,
Like the nightingale in the trees.
Awakening the dawn among the elm groves,
Leaping startled from one branch to another.

O my sacred, Portuguese guitar!
O poet who composes verses without fear,
Trilling, out of love, in life without secrets
Your poems bewitch the river's waters!

Cease your roar, then, you pure singing rivers
As you surge down the hard stone,
Listen to my graceful guitar.

The guitar laments, the poetry implores,
Murmuring dreams of great beauty,
Times of passion in the poet's life.

Lembrando

Lembrando quantas vezes percorri
Os lindos caminhos da minha aldeia
Relembro o seu luar da lua cheia
As fadas que amei e nunca esqueci.

A minha infância contigo vivi
Humilde povo que à luz da candeia
Muita vez comias uma frugal ceia
És o mais fiel que eu conheci.

Mas o tempo passa, fugiram os anos
Cada um de nós viveu desenganos,
Desde a juventude, desde a mocidade.

Por tudo isso aqui neste simples verso,
Meu coração diz a todo o Universo,
De vós, minha gente, é grande a saudade.

Remembering

Remembering how many times I travelled along
The lovely roads of my village
I recall the full moon's moonlight
And the enchanting girls I loved and have never forgotten.

I lived my childhood here with you,
Humble people often eating
Your frugal supper by candlelight,
The most honest people I've ever known.

But time passes, the years take flight,
Each of us has known disappointment
From the time we were young, as we grew up.

For all that's found here in this simple verse
My heart speaks out to the whole Universe
Of how great is my longing for you, my people.

TRANSLATIONS BY HUGH HAZELTON

NELIA BOTELHO

Moon Jelly
(Aurelia labiata, Vancouver Aquarium)

The moon jelly is vagabond
beachcomber
drifter

At moon's mercy
improvising with each current
it tolls a silent bell-shaped body
unfurls its umbrella
with limbs glowing and careless

Evolved as a heartbeat
thin membrane hides nothing
requires neither loadstar nor lighthouse
on a chartless course

It is mariner
astronomer
wanderer
who calls no place home

The Garden Weaver

(Araneus diadematus)

silk filament wrung from the body
a long drawn-out song
of concentric verses
shrill as silver strings
roped in a shroud knot and cast

a blithe sail between brambles
one thin leg anchors the signal line
                    waits—

where blackberries bait
each globe a swollen
bruised lip

and then   the timbre
frequency of distress
the orb holds fast
as a bluebottle
raises and lowers its trilling wings

HUMBERTO DA SILVA

My Starling

Late spring, when I was nine, my cousins and I were playing some varia-
tion of cops and robbers in the street. We noticed a young starling flying
perilously close to the ground. It crashed into a chain link fence and fell,
momentarily stunned. We ran to catch it. The mother bird flew around us
chattering in panic. The fledgling recovered and managed to fly to the top
of the fence. Without even thinking we picked up rocks. We all seemed to
know that this bird was attainable. I threw one of those perfect throws. I can
still see the stone sailing through the air. It brought the starling down. We
captured it. There was blood in its beak and something wrong with its wing.
We argued over whether to kill it, and how. Stone it. Drown it. Throw it
against the wall. We couldn't agree so then we argued over who would get
to keep it. Finally I got it because it was my yard and I had brought it down.
I mended its wing with masking tape and a popsicle stick. I fed it bread
soaked in milk. I kept it on the back porch in a covered box with air holes.
A week later it seemed better so I took off the splint. But I still kept it in the
dark box. One day I opened the box and the starling flew out. It flew to
the top of some old bookshelves on the porch. It flew there because it was
the only place where I could not reach it. I tried to hit it with a broom stick
and accidentally knocked from the shelf an old china teapot my mom used
to water her African violets. It broke. My father came to see what the noise
was and opened the porch door. The starling flew straight out. Sometimes
I would see it on the telephone lines in the yard. Maybe it was taunting me.
No matter how many rocks I threw, I never hit it again.

––––––––––

My mother and father were good to me. Upon me flowed all the love and material comfort they could afford. Innocently they competed to see who could love me more, who could go further to please me. I wasn't spoiled or anything like that. I grew up with a good moral compass. We went to church on Sundays and ate dinner together almost every night. They talked to me about drugs and sex when they thought it was time. I was the focus of their world. They weren't really there for each other. They were there for me.

When I was twelve I got a BB gun for Christmas. It wasn't under the Christmas tree, but in the basement by the furnace chimney where Santa had purportedly left it. My mother didn't talk to my father at all that Christmas. She hated the gun. I loved it. I had first seen it in a display case at Canadian Tire. I wanted it so badly I had harassed my father since June to get it for me. It was the only thing I had ever wanted. It was a Daisy—a boy's first gun. When I got it my father made a big show of explaining some basic rules and told me that if I ever broke those rules he would take away the gun. He told me sternly: it is not a toy. Don't ever point it at another person. Walk with it pointing at the sky or at the dirt. Don't keep it loaded when you aren't using it. Don't load it unless you intend to shoot something. Don't point it at anything you don't intend to shoot. Keep the safety on until you are ready to shoot. He told me not to shoot at pets or domestic animals. But he never said not to kill anything. In fact there was an understanding that that was precisely what the gun was for: to taste the pleasure of killing. We lived in a new suburb at the edge of the city. I would ride my old bike out to a nearby stand of woods and try to kill squirrels, raccoons and cats, but the gun wasn't powerful enough. I looked forward to other Christmases and birthdays where maybe I could get a pump-up pellet gun and maybe even a real .22 rifle. One summer afternoon I came upon two sparrows having a dust bath beside the road. Like the expert rifleman I had become I shoul-dered the Daisy and squeezed a quick shot. One of the sparrows tumbled into a heap of dusty brown feathers. The other flew off in a terrified flutter. When I picked up the shot sparrow it was warm and limp. There was blood in its beak. When it blinked I dropped it on the road, terrified. Then I shot it again. In its breast. Point blank.

Then commenced the slaughter. Sparrows by the dozens, starlings, robins, chickadees. Once a blue jay. Birds that sang and birds that didn't. I shot a few pigeons, but they were hard to kill. No matter how good a shot, they would fly off wounded. Even if you chased and shot them again, they might not die. I shot birds all the time, even in the spring when my father said it wasn't right. He said I might shoot a bird that had nestlings waiting somewhere, and that was a sin. I begged him for a better gun for my birthday, but got a Hot Wheels track instead. I begged again at Christmas and got a new bike. Eventually I stopped killing birds all the time. I got into other things. But for a long time, every time I saw a bird, I would calculate the windage, the distance, and the trajectory of the shot.

When I was seventeen, I fell in love for the first time. It was an amazing and confusing feeling; it was like a falling dream where suddenly you are flying. I ached with love but had no comprehension of why someone could love me. And with love came feelings that tormented me: the need to possess, the fear of losing love. My girlfriend could not understand why I was so insecure and why it made me so cruel. I did not know where those feelings came from either but I started to destroy my love with them. I cast ugly words at her like stones. I denied her my feelings. Finally I broke her heart with a string of petty betrayals intended to demonstrate she didn't matter to me. She had to quit high school in her final year to get away from me. Then she betrayed me in turn by getting over me and finding herself a college boyfriend with a car. I don't think that in her understanding this constituted a betrayal, but I knew better. I was devastated. But I knew that was how it should be. First love never works out.

One morning after a night of competitive drinking at a university friend's cottage, I took a Crossman pneumatic air rifle for a walk in the woods. My friend, whose rifle it was, said that although the manufacturer suggested you only pump the rifle ten times, you could pump it twenty times if you wanted to kill something bigger. I pumped it twenty times before inserting the fat .22 pellet in the breech. In the brush I startled two mourning doves that flew high into a budding oak. It was spring. I watched the doves for a few minutes. They forgot I was there and one began a mating display. I aimed at both doves in turn, then selected the lover as my victim. I didn't know if I would make the shot as it would certainly have been out of range for my Daisy. Over one hundred feet straight up. I took the shot. The dove lifted gently from its perch. It hung momentarily in the air. Then it dropped from branch to branch, wings limp, and fell ten feet in front of me. The second dove did not fly away, and I felt no need to shoot it. I walked to the dead bird and picked it up. It was limp. It had been a beautiful creature in its life. Then it was mine.

My first real lie was to my best friend. I did it to protect his feelings, or that's what I told myself. I told him I wasn't sleeping with a mutual ex-girlfriend when I was. I figured I had a right to sleep with her because she was my girlfriend first, and he got her on the rebound. I didn't like lying to him. Lying to your best mate wasn't like lying to your girlfriend. Sometimes you had to lie to your girlfriend. You had to lie to your girlfriend about other girls sometimes. You shouldn't have to lie to your friends about girls. In fact, one of life's pleasures has always been telling your friends about girls. Of course you didn't always tell them everything, especially not about serious girlfriends. In fact, one of the things you didn't tell them is how serious a girlfriend sometimes is. That's kind of how I got to the point of having to lie to my friend. He kept asking me if I was serious about my/our girlfriend. I kept telling him it wasn't that serious. Actually, I didn't think it was that serious. He actually asked me once if it would be okay with me if he slept with my girlfriend. I actually told him: sure it was okay. Of course I could tell him this because I didn't actually believe that it would happen. But then it did. I had already broken off with her. It was just getting a little too serious, I needed a little distance, and what do you think happened? Two weeks into the separation my best friend and my very recently dumped ex-girlfriend are like a house on fire. I saw it coming and I didn't. I knew it was happening and I didn't. So then I did the tour of emotions: fuck him, fuck her, I don't give a fuck, I'll just fuck someone else, oh fuck. Then I wanted her back. Bad. I wanted her like I never wanted her before. I made myself into everything that she had ever wished I was. I spoke to her of love when the mere mention of the word in our relationship had heretofore given me hives. I was forced to face up to the fact that maybe I had loved her after all. After a river of tears and some laughter, we were an item again. But my best friend was there too. But me and my ex-ex, well, it just seemed so right . . .I lost interest in her shortly after he did. But for a while, there we were, living a Bizarre Love Triangle. It would have been funny, or exciting, or something if I didn't have to lie to my best friend. When you can lie to your best friend, you can lie to anybody.

After I married, my wife and I would wedge in a holiday every summer at my father-in-law's vineyard in Alentejo, Portugal. He had retired there to twenty hectares of Trincadeira grapes that he turned into fairly good wine, and he made a little money doing it. The peace of the place was marred by one thing. He had a propane-powered scarecrow device that fired what sounded like a gunshot every minute or so. He said it was the only effective way to keep the goddamned birds off the grapes. He also had an old Beretta semi-auto twelve gauge behind the side door. Sometimes I would take the gun and a few shells and go for a walk around the vineyards. It felt great to walk around property that I could anticipate one day being mine. It felt even better to do it holding a loaded shotgun. Employed, married, enfranchised, armed with a real gun; I was at last truly all grown up. I would count the seconds from the last propane discharge and fire the gun at the same time. I killed a few things: a rat, a rabbit once, but it wasn't really hunting.

One day when I was out walking with the gun, the sky above me suddenly darkened with pigeons. There were hundreds of them swirling and diving to take turns feasting on the remnant wheat from a neighbour's freshly harvested field. Without thinking I raised the gun. I fired blindly into the roiling flock above me. I fired until the gun was empty. Pigeons fell about me like a biblical curse, some dead, some still living. I walked from pigeon to pigeon, examining each one. I wasn't sure what I should do about the ones that were still alive. I didn't have any more shells and administering a twelve-gauge coup de grâce to a pigeon seemed ludicrous. I should break their necks, I thought. But I knew I couldn't do it. It was too . . . intimate. Finally I walked back to the house. I left the gun and returned with a garden spade. Not many of the pigeons were still alive but I swiftly brought down the edge of the spade across the necks of those that were, decapitating them. Then I dug shallow graves to hold them, lest my new family should discover my bloodlust.

"What were you shooting at?" my wife asked.

I lied. "A rabbit."

"Did you get it?"

"No."

"Good. If you like shooting why don't you take up skeet?"

"It's not about shooting."

"No? Then what is it about?"

"It's about the vestigial hunting instinct. It's about walking your domain with a weapon and taking what you need. It's a man thing."

"Did you ever eat anything you killed?"

I didn't have to think about it. "No."

"And it's not about shooting?"

I thought about it. "No."

"Then it's about killing. And that's sad."

"It's not about killing," I said, knowing for once I was telling her the truth.

Five years into our marriage our first child was born. It was the child we thought we needed to fulfill the promise of a marriage which had quickly become a routine of career, control, and comfort. We thought a child would fill the hole. Seeing my daughter born was the most emotional moment of my life. I was filled with the prototypical joy and wonder. That morning when I left the hospital, each birdsong was a note of intense beauty. All the love I had inside of me gelled for my beautiful child. But there was none left over for anyone else.

My wife grew up in a home where it was barely concealed that her father cheated on her mother. My wife's older sister married early and unhappily. Their younger brother is gay, if that has anything to do with anything. My wife always said that she would never be so fettered by convention that she could not leave a marriage soiled by dishonesty. She always told me that she was with me only because of her choice to be with me, and that her choice could change at any moment. She refused to swear 'til death do us part.' And I was okay with that.

My daughter's first years were spent in a home with a father who loved her and a mother who loved her, but that was sterile in every other way. My daughter took over my wife's life. Work and adultery soon took over mine. The marriage had become that sort of modern theatre where the audience and the characters mingle and interact. Many times I thought of leaving to find something more authentic, but I had no clue as to what that would be. My wife did. One day she was there but I knew she was gone. I was devastated, but what could anyone expect in a time where pretty much fifty percent of marriages end in divorce.

When I left my house I stayed at my father's place for a while. My parents had separated shortly after I had gotten my first real job. When I wasn't working I would spend hours in his yard catatonic but for the actions required to smoke. The yard backed onto a ravine and was filled with every species of local bird: cardinals, jays, woodpeckers, chickadees. I watched them, and listened, and wondered if they knew who I was. In the evening the birdsong was so precious that it made me cry for everything I had ever lost. When I caught myself distractedly doing the math for a shot, I was filled with the most profound loathing for myself. I sobbed. I made myself promise never to kill another living thing for as long as I lived.

When my daughter was ten I tried to teach her how to shoot. We were weekending at a mutual friend's cottage and my ex-wife and I were in the "see we can be friends" stage of our divorce. I had borrowed a child-sized BB gun from the neighbour's boy, who happened to be out shooting birds. I set up a row of tin cans on a fence and tried to teach her how to sight in the gun, breathe and squeeze the trigger. She had the eagle eye, like me, and was plinking off the cans in no time but she had absolutely no interest in shooting. She was simply trying to please me. When my ex-wife came back from town and saw what we were doing, she pulled me aside with a clenched smile and demanded to know what the hell I thought I was doing. I told her I was teaching our daughter to shoot. That it didn't mean anything. She told me that if I ever put a gun in her daughter's hands again, it would be the last time I saw her. I was surprised by the strident attitude my ex-wife was taking. Stupidly, I told her it was just a BB gun, a kid's gun, and I was just teaching her how to handle it safely. She told me, in a voice colder than anything I had heard from her through the discoveries, recriminations, and the divorce, that there wasn't any way to handle any gun safely. They weren't meant to be safe.

My daughter starts high school this year. She is a beautiful young woman with something of an artistic sensibility. She likes to draw. Right now all she draws are hands and feet in perfect painstaking detail. You can actually tell whose feet or hands they are if you know the individual. She can render their immutable characteristics. She can perfectly capture every flaw. She just doesn't like to draw the whole creature. I have asked her to draw birds for me but she says she can't draw things that won't stay still. I know she can do it because she has sketched them offhandedly in art class. I saved those drawings from her trove of juvenilia and treasure. I offer to buy her some birds to be her subjects, but she refuses. She says she doesn't ever want to draw anything kept in a cage. I ask her to draw birds from telephoto pictures I have taken. She said I don't need a drawing of something I have already photographed. I do not understand her obstinacy. One day, Dad, one day. I wish I could get through to her and make her understand how much it would mean to me for her to draw me a starling on a wire.

I sort of kept my promise. I have killed flies, mosquitoes, cockroaches. I trapped a mouse and cried when I found that the trap had done its work, leaving the tiny creature broken and still. But I never again killed anything for the pleasure of killing it. For the most part the love in my life has unfolded as a series of mistakes, or maybe the same mistake oft-repeated. The rampage of bad relationships before and after my failed marriage never really bothered me. I could never fully appreciate something until I destroyed it. Besides, I already had the only relationship I ever truly wanted. Everything else was sport, or convenience. But my love for my daughter is pure and it is the one promise that I have never broken. It sustained me. It was my absolution. It meant everything to have someone in the world to who you never needed to lie.

Late one spring, when I was nine, I found a starling with a broken wing. It must have been a fledgling on one of its first forays from the nest. It flew into the middle of the road and a car ran over it. It tumbled in the turbulence beneath the vehicle and broke a wing. I took it home and mended the wing with masking tape and a popsicle stick. I fed it bread soaked in milk. I kept my starling in a box on the back porch. By the end of the week my starling would sit on the edge of the box and sing when the sun rose. She was a funny-looking bird with its wing taped and splinted like it was, but it had a beautiful song. After the second week I took off the splint and the tape. Now my starling would sit on the edge of the box and try its wings while it sang. One day I found that my starling had flown to the top of some old bookshelves beside a window in the back porch. My starling sang its song to the other starlings. Soon it would not come down from the shelves. I could no longer feed it by hand. I would just leave food in the box. One day I opened the porch door and my starling flew away. Before disappearing it alighted on the telephone line that cut across the yard. It looked about and sang. I was sad and happy. Until that autumn my starling always returned to the telephone wire to sing. I could always tell it was her by the funny wing.

CLEMENTE ALVES

Confessions of an Altar Boy

Pork, Porkchop, Pork & Cheese and Chop. Welcome to me. Welcome to the Porkchop Kid from Little Portugal. *Bacalhau* for lunch and dinner every Friday. The rosary every night. Beatings in Portuguese school while normal kids played ball hockey. Welcome to life as a *Porkinho* in Toronto's Portuguese *bairro*.

In the early 1980s, Little Portugal was about one hundred thousand strong—one of the largest Portuguese communities in all of North America. Its size and concentration kept the Portuguese language and traditions from assimilating into the Canadian population. Decades later, many live and die in the Portuguese ghetto without ever having to learn a single word of English. So strong is the culture of the old country, a culture dominated by its religion, that the de facto centre of the community is the parish church and the priest its undisputed leader. In the bloody heart of Little Portugal sat the Catholic fortress known as the Igreja de Nossa Senhora de Fátima (Church of Our Lady of Fátima), the parish See from whence ruled the religious overlord Senhor Padre Costa. Costa was the last of the Portuguese Grand Inquisitors, a prime product of the Salazarist church. He was born and educated in the powerful, ultra-conservative bishopric of Braga, also known as the Portuguese Rome. In the mid-1960s Costa was sent to Canada to administer the fascist doctrine of *Fado, Fátima & Futebol* to the fast-growing number of Portuguese ex-patriots in Toronto. Padre Costa was a gifted preacher and soon found success as moral dictator over his flock of faithful serfs, his spiritual stranglehold near total and intolerant of any dissent. Even Portuguese atheists went to church, and in the parish of Nossa Senhora the atheists prayed for Christ's protection against the damning purges of the almighty Padre Costa. To ensure the good Lord's attention, they would, of course, place a little extra in the collection basket.

When I was about ten years old, Padre Costa put the call out for altar boys, and so my father offered up his first-born son into the holy service that every proud Catholic kid should humbly complete. There was no use complaining about it. My father simply wrapped his knuckles around the good old Portuguese Belt of Wrath and that ended all arguments. Over the next few weeks, under the strict supervision of Padre Costa, I attended Altar Boy Academy, which consisted of a few hours a week of training and memorizing of terms, tools and rituals, along with a practical lesson or two of actual service. Altar boys in training would serve the evening masses on weekdays, learning the ropes, jingling the bells. These were solemn masses, poorly attended.

On a cold miserable night, after the worst day at school ever, I took refuge in the church. No old women in black around so I had the opportunity to pray in privacy. I prayed—actually I *begged* that God and the Holy Mother would save me from the fat bullies who chased me through the alleyways. I asked them to save me from Mr. Qim, the French teacher from hell who hated my guts and would use Korean army torture techniques to spice up detention. I prayed my parents would not find out about the magnificent F-minus I had just gotten on my math exam.

I prayed and prayed and prayed until the very sky ripped open above me and I was sucked into a wondrous vortex. And so it was that the Angel of the Lord appeared unto me as a pillar of light, and the Angel spoke to me in tongues known only in the heavens, and bestowed upon me the glorious revelation that indeed *I was a Chosen One of God!* Filled with religious fervour, I would go forth and serve the Lord my God as a lowly altar boy until the day my true mission and purpose were at last revealed to me by a burning bush on Mount Sinai or in a bat cave in France. I pledged to be the best damn altar boy the world had ever seen. God was intrigued. *Another minion to test.*

And so came the day that Padre Costa summoned me, the Chosen One of God, for special altar boy duty. A dull school day afternoon was interrupted when the principal's office informed me and this other Chosen One,

Mario, that we had been especially selected by Padre Costa to spontaneously serve at a funeral. Neither of us had ever served a funeral before.

Off we went.

The previous week I had been introduced to foreshadowing and symbolism in English class. I sensed them both waiting in ambush up ahead. We walked out of the school, turned the corner and there it was: the Igreja de Nossa Senhora de Fátima. Her dull Victorian façade took on the shape of a dark gothic cathedral. I saw the gargoyles licking their fangs as we ascended the front steps. My spidey senses tingled. This was going to be a job for Job. Inside the church we found Padre Costa with a list of preparations. His first commandment: *Thou shalt change into thy robes.* So we slipped into the back, into the altar boy vestuary. Despite its fancy name, the vestuary was nothing more than a storage space for church paraphernalia like crosses, candle holders, incense burners, holy water, and so on. It was also home to the church's crowning glory: the sombre, queen-like statue of its patron saint, Nossa Senhora de Fátima herself.

The statue had been imported from Portugal. It was commissioned by Padre Costa, paid for by his parishioners, and shipped over to Canada on a freighter sometime in the late 1960s. She was made of wood, about five feet tall, and dressed in a white gown which covered her from top to toe. On her head, like St. Peter's dome, sat a large silver crown and from her clasped hands hung a long silver rosary. Praying at her exposed feet were the three shepherd children, the seers of Fátima: Francisco, Jacinta and Lúcia. All of them were perched on a sturdy platform that could be carried by strong faithful men.

Mario and I opened the altar boy-designated closet. The robes in the closet had been there for years and were all too big for us. Our own robes were at home. We hadn't planned on serving a funeral when the day began. We chose two of the smaller robes and slipped them on only to be engulfed in fumes of sweat and mildew. There were also two ropes that we tied around our waists—humble belts that sculpted our boyish figures into that much desired monkish look. One was a standard white rope, which Mario nabbed instantly, and the other was a flaming disco-silver whip straight out of purgatory. I put it on and checked myself out in the mirror. I looked like the religious reject from the Village People, the sad skinny friar who wasn't allowed in the navy or stay at the YMCA. Mario insisted I looked fine. In fact, Mario suggested I try on Nossa Senhora's silver crown and rosary to match my shiny silver belt.

Padre Costa entered the room, saving the smiling little bastard from a punch in the teeth. The Padre was breathing heavily and wiped his brow of sweat. He was nervous. I had never seen the grande Padre nervous before. That made me nervous. What did Padre Costa have to be nervous about? A stupid funeral should be no problem for him. No sweat, right? So what's he sweating about? God, he was making me nervous.

Finally he spoke. The deceased and his guests had arrived, he announced. They were waiting for the ceremony to begin. Mario and I were to follow the Padre out onto the altar and flank him, then simply listen to the ceremony and perform our duties as per our training. Unfortunately the Padre had neglected to teach us a single thing about funerals. Nothing. NADA!

When we told him this, the Padre stood there, frozen, staring at us. If looks could kill, then Mario and I had just been impaled and gutted. There was a terrible taste in my mouth and I swear it was the mucus and bile from my own spleen. Padre Costa braced himself against the doorway as his knees seemed to buckle beneath him. He said something, barely audible. Mario and I looked at each other. We didn't understand. Costa mumbled again, his voice weak and quivering. Still we didn't understand, so I asked him.

"Excuse me Senhor Padre, but . . . what did you say?"

"MERDA!" said the Padre.

The Padre said "MERDA!" Dear God! If Padre Costa could swear like that, against every moral lesson he had ever taught me, then could the Apocalypse be far behind? I could feel Satan's hot rancid breath on the back of my neck. My soul had been corrupted, perhaps irreversibly, and still all the Padre could say was *"Merda. Merda. Merda!"*

Mario tried to break Padre Costa out of his trance by approaching him and reaching out. The Padre swatted his big hairy hand at Mario, barely missing his nose and batting a poor innocent fly out of thin air. My wide unbelieving eyes followed the tiny, pulverized corpse bullet as it flew towards the Nossa Senhora—splat—giving her a well-defined nipple of black and green goo on her left boob. "Get back you miserable wretch," Costa growled at Mario in Portuguese. "Don't touch me!"

But good on Mario because the Padre stood up straight and regained his composure. He cleared his throat and spoke once again. We were to stay close to him and listen carefully for his instructions. His orders would be whispered discreetly so that no one would be the wiser. This was a very important funeral, he said, and he didn't want anything to go wrong. *Wrong? I thought. What could possibly go wrong?* The Padre turned to exit, but with his back towards us he spoke again.

"I'm counting on you boys to make me look good. But I'm warning you, don't let me down, or so help me God, you will curse the day you ever set foot on that altar."

The terrible taste of mucus and bile was back. I so wanted to puke. Actually, I did puke, but only a small mouthful that I somehow managed to swallow back into the toxic depths of my twisted, seething bowels. But wait, that's not the gross part. The Padre left. We were supposed to follow. Mario motioned to me but I insisted that he go first and thankfully he obliged because just then . . . I farted.

I couldn't help it. My innards grow explosively unstable under extreme stress. It was a huge, horrible fart. By far the most terrible smell ever smelt. The shear terribleness made me want to puke again so I quickly exited the vestuary and shut the door, trapping the fart, leaving it to fester and froth and wait like a sinister backdraft for that unsuspecting waft of fresh air to ignite it. Then the fart, like a ravenous ball of demonic fire, would merci-lessly devour all in its wake. Safe on the other side, with my back against the door, I took a deep sweet breath, relaxed just enough, then off I went to serve the funeral.

We entered the church from a doorway next to the altar. The deceased and his entourage of thirty men and women, all dressed in their finest black, were waiting for us. I didn't recognize any of them but I assumed by the way the Padre was behaving that they were all VIPs: Very Important Portuguese. At the foot of the altar sat the coffin. I stared at it, fascinated by the fact that inside was a body. A dead body. Wow! The person in that fancy box was dead. But the coffin was closed, so then I began wondering if there was a body inside at all. How did they know? Maybe it was someone else's body? Maybe it was a zombie? Or a vampire even? Yeah, that's it, a vampire! How did they know that Dracula himself wasn't lying in there, all comfy in his bed of Transylvanian dirt, just dying to be buried in the family tomb so that at night by the light of the full moon he could rise from the ghastly sleep of the undead and start sucking everybody's blood? Good God! Dracula was going to suck all the Portuguese dry. The horror! They should open that coffin. Open it, damnit, open it!

Mario kicked me in the shin.

"Ow! You mother . . ."

"Wake up, Porko!" he whispered. "We've got a funeral to serve."

"Yeah I know," I growled. "Dracula's funeral."

Mario looked at me funny and scrunched his face. "What's that smell?"

Padre Costa began the ceremony. Costa, I must say, was a master orator. Like all fine despots, he knew how to lull and stir a crowd with the perfect alchemy of words and gestures. He had a big bombastic voice yet he worked subtle inflection with ease. However, his secret weapon was his beautiful singing voice. If music is known to soothe the savage beast, for Padre Costa, music *served* the beast so it was only natural that he began the ceremony with a ritual chant, sung of course in that all-purpose mock Gregorian melody that priests seem to love so much. It was a powerful opening. The maestro was on stage. As the ceremony continued, Costa grew stronger and more confident. The friends and family of the dearly departed were definitely getting their money's worth. Their sorrow and grief appeared to lift from their faces as Costa, the good news anchor and spiritual shepherd of God, worked his sheep-herding magic on their needy souls.

And Mario and I? We were flawless. Padre Costa whispered his instructions to us and we performed our duties with poise and expertise. It was like a symphony: Costa played us like violins and we sang in harmony. It was easy. I was the best damn altar boy the world had ever seen! Padre Costa ended his sermon. Silence echoed through the church. The Padre fixed his eyes on the faces of his sombre audience, assuring their eyes were fixed on him. At the very second when the silence could be tolerated no longer, the Padre began to sing. The man had perfect pitch. The Very Important Portuguese took their cue and joined the sing-along. Then Costa turned and walked back to the head of the altar. His eyes shifted from side to side, looking for something. He motioned for Mario and I to approach.

"Okay, incense. I need the incense. Where's the censer?"

Mario and I looked around. No censer. "Uh . . . in the vestuary," I told him.

"What the hell is it doing there? I need it here!"

I just shook my head and shrugged my shoulders.

"Well, go and get it, *pateta!* What are you waiting for? *Zash!*"

Pateta. My priest had just called me a pateta.

Pateta is the Portuguese word for idiot, fool, dufus, loser, nimrod, jerk, stupid, ignoramus, bafoon, moron, gimp, goof and gork. And a few other colourful adjectives I'm sure I'm leaving out. In Portuguese, one magical word like pateta can say oh so much.

I approached the vestuary. My hand reached for the doorknob. Slowly, I turned the doorknob. The door creaked open. Foolishly I entered the ill-fated chamber. There was a ghostly whisper of churning gases, of volatile chemistries, and a split second later, I was swallowed like Jonah. Swallowed alive! He by the whale, I by the whale fart. It was as if I had taken a boot to the stomach. I couldn't breathe. I gagged, gasped for precious molecules. Tears spewed from my eyes, squeezed out of my body by the fiery gas.

I fashioned an instant gas mask with my robe and covered my face, only to be punched in the nose by the pungent product of altar boy sweat glands from as far back as 1973. I was gonna pass out and puke again. *What irony this! Killed . . . killed by my own fart.*

I needed fresh oxygen, hydrogen, anything—the window! If I could get to the window and open it, I'd be saved. The glass panes, grimy with dust, was partially covered by a massive shelf cluttered with church stuff. I dragged over a chair, hopped on, pushed the golden censer aside and left it teetering on the edge. I reached for the window latch through the jumble of candles and candle holders, crosses, chalices, plastic bags of Holy Hosts, jugs of holy water, and six bottles of wine. Six dusty bottles of Jesus juice. The wine instantly conjured up memories of my father and uncles back in the Azores, testing my manhood with *"só um beijinho"* (a little kiss) from a glass of port or some horrible homemade *vinho tinto* at the dinner table. I don't know why I did it. Maybe it was the devil, but I needed a drink. With the robe still covering most of my face, I reached for the one bottle that was half empty, pulled out the cork and took a swig. Then I choked and coughed and spat it right back out. It burned the inside of my mouth and dribbled off my chin. This wasn't wine, it was *aguardente!* Fire water! What the hell was fire water doing in the bottles supposed to contain the Blood of Christ?

I quickly returned the aguardente to the shelf, and that's when I saw the hockey pucks. Twelve hockey pucks, round, black, stacked one on top of another, in four orderly piles. I looked around for some corresponding hockey sticks but nope, just hockey pucks. Distracted by that discordant sight among the religious effects, I forgot about the murderous contagion aloft in the air, dropped the robe covering my mouth and inhaled, deeply. I was shocked and stunned by the awful lingering power of the evil fart. I hacked as if stabbed in the lung. I stumbled off the chair, spun around, tripped on the hem of my giant robe, and knocked over the big golden censer I had been sent to retrieve. My head hit the floor, and the big stupid thing landed upon my face. I swiped at the blood streaming from the deep gash on my forehead and shook off the cartoon tweety birds circling round my cranium. I looked up, and towering above me was the statue of Nossa Senhora, all white and heavenly, looking down so sweetly.

"Nossa Senhora," I prayed. "Lady of great miracles. Please get me out of this. If there was ever a time for a miracle, it's now. This is it, baby, you can do it."

But instead of healing my gaping wound or hurling the sun towards the Earth in a planet-smashing death spin, Nossa Senhora simply shook her head and said, "*Pateta.*" Now the Mother of God had called me a pateta.

"What the hell?" Mario was standing in the doorway. His shocked, prepubescent, testosterone-challenged voice cracked. "What did you do?"

"The Nossa Senhora just called me a pateta."

"What!? What the . . .what the hell is that smell!?" Mario took a step back. "Dude, what kind of *feijão* does your mother feed you for breakfast?"

"The Nossa Senhora called me a pateta," I said again. But Mario was on a mission. He was there to get the incense and no whacked-out altar boy or a smell from hell was going to thwart his design.

"Look," he said forcefully. "Costa wants the incense and he's boiling mad. I swear I saw red devil eyes behind those Mr. Magoo goggles of his. Where's the censer? Hey! I'm talking to you!"

"Here!" I said, wiping the blood snaking down my face. "The censer thing is here." I picked it up off the floor and handed it to him.

"There's blood on it! What the hell, man?"

"The stupid thing fell on my head!"

"Alright, keep it down. You've screwed things up enough already. Where's the incense? Inside?"

He opened the little metal hatch and peered into the censer. "It's just a bunch of ash. Where's the incense?"

I stood up and tried to clean myself off as best I could. Blood was trailing down my forehead, trying to bleed its way back into my body through my eyeball. Mario turned to the shelf and began searching.

"Don't bother," I told him. "There's nothing but *aguardente* and hockey pucks."

"Hockey pucks? What hockey pucks?"

"There," I pointed out.

Mario picked one up and sniffed. "These aren't hockey pucks, you bloody idiot. This is the incense!"

"What? Let me see that." I plucked the thing out of his hand and took a sniff. "Oh. Well . . . it looks like a friggin' hockey puck!"

"Hockey pucks don't break like this." He demonstrated by effortlessly breaking the thing in half. I was astonished by the endless depths of my own stupidity.

"Right," he said, taking complete charge of the situation. "Costa is out there, trying to conduct a funeral, okay? A funeral! Now, how do you get this stuff burning?"

"Rub your skinny legs together and get a spark?"

"Ha ha. So hilarious. Gimme your lighter."

"Don't be stupid," I replied. "You know I quit smoking in Grade 3."

"Forget it," he said as he found a book of matches on the shelf. He set the censer on the table and shoved the pieces of the incense hockey puck into the thing. He ripped out a match, lit it, and threw it into the censer. The flame instantly went out. He tried it again and again but he couldn't get the incense to burn. Mario's stress multiplied exponentially with each and every match that failed. And then Mario set himself on fire.

Mario pinched that fateful match between his fingers and ripped it out. He folded the matchbook backwards and struck the match. It didn't light. He struck it again. Still no good. But the next strike flared like a torch and the matchbook, worn out from all the friction and hot sulphurous activity, exploded in Mario's hands. There are moments in life that are so absurd, so ridiculous, so unbelievably contrary to believability, that when they happen, they appear to happen in slow motion so as to firmly and clearly imprint themselves in your memory forever and ever, amen, making the moment unforgettable and so technicolour real. This was one of those moments. The flaming matches fell to the floor, landed on the hem of Mario's Friar Tuck robe and began a vicious feeding frenzy on those far-out 70s polyester fibres. Mario lit up like a disco ball.

Dear God! Mario's on fire! I must save him!

So, instinctively—which means without any thought whatsoever—I grabbed the first thing with liquid in it, which of course happened to be the bottle of aguardente off the shelf. Mario was freaking out and was spinning around the room, threatening to spread the fire and burn the whole church down. In superfast action I uncorked the bottle and slopped its contents all over him, turning the poor bastard into a human Molotov Cocktail. I splashed some of the aguardente in his eyes and blinded him. It wasn't exactly a scream he let out then, but rather a screech, a blood-curdling, ear-piercing screech, fuelled with inhuman pain, like that of an infant boy having his foreskin chopped off. Realizing my mistake, I dropped the bottle on the floor, shattering it, and grabbed one of the jugs of Holy Water. I poured the cool salvationous water over poor flaming Mario, finally dousing the fire and ending the terrible scene.

I had saved Mario. I had saved the life of another Chosen One with a badass baptism of fire. I was the best damn altar boy the world had ever seen!

Mario stood there, drenched, flabbergasted. I believe he was in shock. So was I. To be perfectly honest, he wasn't really hurt. The bottom half of his robe and pants were scorched, but the only burns he suffered that day were to his psyche, not his skin. And maybe *that* was the miracle I had been praying so hard for during my rapture.

On cue, Padre Costa burst into the vestuary, eyes flaming, nostrils flaring, jaws clenching. He must have been doing backflips in an attempt to stall for time while his all-star altar boys tag-teamed the incense. Waiting, singing and sweating before hearing the screams from the vestuary. The family and friends of the deceased, those Very Important Portuguese, must have been horrified. They must have wondered what house of horrors this priest was running, and indeed if all the rumours about the rogue Padre were true after all? And what does he find but two dumb, shell-shocked altar boys—one with an empty jug of holy water in his hand, a broken bottle of aguardente by his feet and blood pouring from his forehead, and the other soaked to the bone, stinking of burnt polyester and 120 proof alcohol, in a room filled with smoke.

"What the hell is going on here?" His eyelids were peeled back in ire, revealing blood-shot eyes magnified by thick spectacles. "You!" He focused his laser beam gaze upon Mario. "You were supposed to bring me the incense, goddamnit!" He swung his freaky eyes back to me. "And you—" He stopped suddenly and clasped a hand over his nose. He stumbled backwards as if pushed by an evil invisible force.

I had farted again.

Desperately I looked up to the Nossa Senhora for comfort and guidance, for deliverance! My heart began beating like a piston, filling my extremities with fevered blood. Surely she, under direct orders from God, would take pity on me and save me. Save *us*. This time she had to, she was going to, I could feel it. But once again she shook her wooden head, rolled her merciless eyes, and upon all three of us she delivered Her word.

"*Patetas.*"

TONY CORREIA

One Man's Island

Vancouver hatches plan for backyard chickens

*The City of Vancouver has moved one step closer to
allowing urban chicken coops in residential backyards.
Councillors voted unanimously on Thursday night to direct
staff to study the issue and draft a bylaw amendment.*
FRIDAY, MARCH 6, 2009
CBC News

No one witnessed my father transport the chickens into the Canadian Tire
shed: they just magically appeared one day. Like God, my father worked in
mysterious ways.

The turquoise tin shed had doubled as a pigeon coop for years. The only
pets permitted on our premises were a potential source of protein. It was
summer 1978. I was too young to get a job but old enough to be embarrassed
by my Portuguese parents.

"Kakadoodledoooooooo!"

The nearest chicken in Brampton, Ontario, was at the plant nearly a mile
away. I sat up in bed and looked at my rolodex clock radio. Had I turned it
on in my sleep? Perhaps some DJ was doing his shtick. The numbers on the
clock idly rolled from 6:15 to 6:16, but other than that, dead silence.

"Kakadoodledoooooooo!"

Nope. That was real.

I got out of bed and went downstairs. Mom was in the kitchen with my
brother, Fernando, who was enjoying his cornflakes and coffee—and not in
the complementary sense; Fernando poured coffee *over* his cornflakes.

"Why are you up so early?" he asked.

"You didn't hear that?"

"What?"

"I must be going crazy," I said.

"Kakadoodledoooooooo!"

My mother and brother continued chatting with each other in Portuguese. There was no way they could not have heard that. It had finally happened. My parents' crazy customs had finally pushed me over the edge. I was losing my mind.

The sound of the rooster's caw had come through the kitchen window that looked out on the tin shed in the yard. I went back upstairs to the second floor landing and out the back door in my bare feet. The morning sun reflected off the patio, Mediterranean-like, causing me to squint. I approached the shed with caution and then pressed my eye to the plastic window. There they were: a rooster and three hens. This was crazy, even by Portuguese immigrant standards.

"Kakadoodledoooooooo!"

"When did we get chickens?" I asked my mother and brother when I returned to the kitchen.

Mom had not learned to speak a word of English in the decade or so she had lived in Canada. She pushed up her glasses and looked to my brother for a translation.

"The chickens are new?" he asked her. Fernando worked two or three jobs at a time at all hours of the day and night; days bled into weeks for him. My mother nodded. He turned to me. "I thought we always had chickens."

"What happened to the pigeons?" I asked. Again, my mom listened as Fernando spoke. She responded with a flurry of words.

"They were delicious," Fernando repeated for her.

I thought those chicken legs were kind of small.

Livestock was nothing new to our household but they were usually dead on arrival. By today's standards, my father's activities would be classified as "sustainable" but in the late 70s he was just a capital "I" immigrant. Our house was like the lost city of Kandor, the capital of Krypton, shrunken and stored inside a glass dome in Superman's Fortress of Solitude. The backyard was a scale model of my parents' previous home in São Miguel, Azores. How we had managed to avoid the authorities' notice before our neighbours brought us to their attention was a miracle, no doubt the work of the garden Madonna or any one of the many statues of saints and martyrs that decorated our home.

My father was a man for whom work was leisure. The only time he sat down was to smoke a cigarette, drink a beer or fall asleep in front of the television in his La-Z-boy chair. He ran our house like a farm, and for all intents and purposes it was. My father didn't raise pigs but once a year he slaughtered one. He grew his own fruits and vegetables, made his own wine, stuffed and smoked chorizo. Even in the dead of winter, he grew flowers in a greenhouse he built to get a head start on the coming spring.

The garage doubled as a wine cellar. Right next to the lawn mower and snow blower was my father's vertical wine press that Fernando frequently threatened to squish me in. My father, uncles and brothers would take turns straining against an iron bar, going around in circles to close the wooden plates together, squeezing the juices out of the grapes and down a cast iron spout. The neighbours knew winter was coming from the flies that swarmed the grape crates stacked on the curb next to the garbage. That year's vintage would be aged in green tear-shaped Mateus bottles recycled from weddings and family functions. My role in the winemaking process was to deliver it to our Canadian neighbours like some under-age gin runner. They would take it from me like I had made them an ashtray out of a bird's nest, thanking me politely but not knowing quite what to do with it.

After the wine came the making of *pimenta*, a fermented red pepper paste the Portuguese put on everything, and utilized by my mother as a weapon to keep me from picking my nose. Crates of grapes were replaced with crates of red chili peppers that were cleaned, stemmed and shoved into metal meat grinders. The spicy heat from the peppers would burn through the rubber gloves my mother and sisters wore, getting into the skin, and stinging their faces for days when they absentmindedly rubbed them with their hands. Mason jars of the stuff lined the shelves of our cold storage pantry for the year.

For the grand finale, my father would take my brothers and me to a farm to look at pigs. The first time I went to a pig farm, my father carefully examined the hogs in their pens before picking one out. I thought we were going to bring it home with us in the car but a farmhand pulled out a gun and shot it in the head. Petting zoos were never the same after that. The pig would hang by its hind legs from a hook in the garage for the neighbours to see, its blood draining into plastic buckets for blood sausage. Every piece of that pig was put to use for pork chops, pork roasts, ribs, and broths, which were then stored in the horizontal meat freezer in the laundry room.

The neighbours probably thought they were living next to the Munsters what with all the strange activity and smells coming out of the garage. They'd smile uncomfortably whenever I brought them another plate of chorizo or Portuguese moonshine but they never complained. At least, not to our faces. Maybe that's what emboldened my father to get the chickens.

My friends had thought they had seen everything when I showed them the chickens in the Canadian Tire shed. "Your dad is a weird man."

"I know," I said.

"Do the chickens have names?"

"No. They'll probably end up as dinner."

My family lived in the basement. That's where the TV was, as well as the food and the beer. Upstairs was immaculate, reserved for special occasions, unwrapping Christmas presents, prayers, and sleeping. When friends and relatives came a-calling they used the back door knowing we would hear the doorbell from there. Only strangers and Jehovah's Witnesses used the front doorbell so when it rang, it meant unwanted company.

We'd had the chickens for about a week when my mother and I heard the front doorbell chime during a commercial break of *The Price is Right*. Mom was sitting next to me on the couch, knitting her millionth doily. She looked up at the ceiling over her glasses and tried to drown out the sound with the clicking of her needles. The bell rang again in rapid succession like someone in a hurry. Since Mom feared the front door as much as the English language I took it upon myself to answer it.

The man's suit and hat suggested he was a salesman but he lacked the requisite briefcase and literature.

"Are your parents at home?" he asked.

"Yes," I said. "But they don't speak English."

He rolled his eyes like that explained everything. He must not have noticed the Holy Family mosaic cemented into the grey brick near the front door.

"I'm from the health department," he said. "We've received complaints from your neighbours about the chickens you've been keeping in the backyard. They smell and the noise from the rooster is a nuisance."

"Okay."

"Would you mind telling your parents for me?"

"Sure."

"Thanks." He nodded politely and returned to his car parked by the curb. He cut across our immaculate lawn, an act that was strictly verboten. Had my father been working in his rose garden, he would have sprayed the man with the hose even if he were Trudeau himself.

Mom looked at me wide-eyed for a translation.

"*Galinhas*—the chickens," I tried to tell her in broken Portuguese, flapping my arms like wings. "The neighbours *naõ gosto.*"

It was hopeless. Mom spent the rest of the day on the phone complaining to her Portuguese friends. It wasn't until Fernando came home from work that she got the whole story.

Mom waited until my father had consumed a bowl of soup that he cooled down with homemade wine before telling him about the neighbour's complaints. My father was a man of few words in both his native and adopted tongues. His expression was a mixture of astonishment and betrayal when he realized for the first time that the neighbours were talking about him behind his back. He retired to his La-Z-boy chair, sighed, and was lulled into snoring sleep by the Portuguese news channel.

The next morning the rooster crowed on cue. I cringed at the sound of its voice, afraid of who might come to our door this time, what kind of fine we might face. Then I heard the metal doors of the shed slide open.

"Kakadoodledoooooooo," the rooster cried.

"Kakadoodle—er-er—ack—ack."

The rooster's choking call seemed to go on forever. It was almost comical, cartoonish, like a Muppet being strangled. The hens followed in short order. I often wonder if my father hoped the neighbours were listening, if he was trying to make them feel uncomfortable for making him extinguish this small piece of happiness, this *lembrança* of where he came from, of the man he used to be before he pushed a broom into retirement. It was like he was reminding them that they had blood on their hands too.

In the years that followed, the tradition of making pimenta and chorizo would dwindle as each of my sisters were married off. The winemaking stopped and the press and the barrels disappeared without my noticing.

Now, some twenty years later as cities loosen restrictions on keeping chickens and bees, the same types of people—urban sophisticates—who looked down their noses at my father are embracing his practices. I used to be embarrassed by him because he was a Portuguese hillbilly. As it turned out, my father was just ahead of his time.

IRENE MARQUES

Writing and speaking

What I write is melted salt embedded in dazzling sapphires,
the ones you refused to put on my wrist when I begged you to in the days
when I was young and beautiful and not yet wise—a mere Ariana
at the window of the world unaware of the sleeping powers
under my rich bosom

But now I have melted them, and have done with them, wonders unseen

What I write is born out of mercy, born out of me
every time I cast my eyes across the short window of your world
and insist on throwing rain drops that become lilies and valleys
and high mountains where I ascend to my youth
and fix everything: becoming grand and vast
and never-ending—a bride to forever be

What I write is mere sulfur,
phosphorous bubbling gases springing from the bottom of myself
speaking all I can say with my mouth,
my fingers pulling the elemental letters
that pulsate beneath the seventh ring of the earth's crust,
the place that saw me being born and then die only to become again

I breathe beneath the moon, on the side of the sun
in the middle of Uranus
melting down tear by tear
gas by gas

It's all that I am

I speak and I write
for me and you

In salted letters
love is
the salt that tempers the meals of your day
and makes my limbs walk

Words

words are dripping out of me and I need a bucket
woke up like this, losing myself on the floor

woke up like this, watering the floor of my house
soaked, soaking the wood I move upon
entering the sliding scale of my diluted measure
lost, found, smiling to my own sense
letting my fragility run through my fingers
in freedom, a freedom that makes me reach
reaching my arm out to find a bridge

water syllables with open vowels
washing my mouth, swallowed, spit in incantation
gliding in me like running trains
taking me to the end of the road
taking me to a lighthouse in the vast Atlantic sea
where father is a fisherman, mother praying on the shore
praying he comes back whole, with feet and arms, and eyes steady
to feed us all
the sardines and the cod
the sea salt—the basis for all our meals

words are dripping out of me
I need a bucket
for capture
the body of Christ falling on my feet
I kiss this water, this blood, this moist
soaked, soaking, singing amidst floating arias
becoming the sister and the mother

tearing myself to nonexistence,
a full being raining upon the lovely world
and the camellias that awoke in the night

bring me more vessels for this thing that keeps crying out of me
come fast, bring many, so that we do not waste
what in me lives and saves and loves and washes
bring a bowl or a cask or an old ceramic cup
made by Madrigana,
the goddess of other times,
with her sturdy crafty hands thick like clay,
red as the belly of the earth, the sun in flames
modelling the things that will become

made by Madrigana
while she stood in the middle of hay fields
waving the wave that makes life and feeds children

words are dripping out of me
I need a bucket for capture
or your hands opened in a perfect cup
the repository of what I carry and must give to the world

this lake, this sea that wets our being
giving us the bath we need
to meander among nothingness
or the in-between of hydrangeas
a pure vagabond of colours

AIDA JORDÃO

Funeral in White

In memory of Ana Maria Gracio

Funeral in White was presented in May 1991 at the Women and Live Words Festival produced by the Company of Sirens, at Theatre Passe Muraille, in Toronto. The playwright was supported by the Canada Council for the Arts Explorations program.

Co-directors: Cynthia Grant, Aida Jordão
Music and sound design: Nuno Cristo
Dramaturge: Lina Chartrand
Production assistance: Naomi Campbell, Loree Lawrence

Cast:

Lídia Saragaço	ALBERTINA
Luciano Iogna	CUSTÓDIO, Albertina's lover, Anita's father
	MÁRIO, Albertina's son, Anita's half-brother
Lorraine Pelletier	ANITA, Albertina and Custódio's daughter
Kathy Imrie	INÊS, Custódio's wife
	DONA EUGÉNIA, a neighbour
	CARLOS, mailman and Anita's second fiancé
Lina Garcia	TERESA, Mário's wife
	DONA ROSA, a neighbour
	SUSANA, Mário and Teresa's daughter, Anita's niece
Nuno Cristo	MUSICIAN, SINGER
	VICTOR, Anita's first fiancé

Scene 1   Lisboa, 1940, bedroom

The stage is dark. CUSTÓDIO *and* ALBERTINA *enter quickly. They lie on a bed and it creaks and sighs under their weight. Clothing is loosened. They make love. They do not speak and their breathing is controlled. The bedsprings creak rhythmically.* INÊS *enters the room.* ALBERTINA *and* CUSTÓDIO *continue to make love.* CUSTÓDIO *has an orgasm.*

INÊS:

Quem está aí contigo? Custódio? Who is with you?

CUSTÓDIO:

Que disparate, mulher! Estava a descansar.

CUSTÓDIO *sits up, and turns on the bedside light.* INÊS *is facing the bed.* ALBERTINA *is lying on the bed, very still.* CUSTÓDIO *gets up and moves away from the bed.* INÊS *follows his movements with her body.*

CUSTÓDIO:

E o jantar? Vamos, Inês, vamos.

CUSTÓDIO *moves past* INÊS *and signals to* ALBERTINA *to follow him. He exits.* INÊS *turns to follow the sounds of his footsteps. She stands silently and listens.* ALBERTINA *doesn't move.* INÊS *makes a sudden move toward the bed but trips on* ALBERTINA's *shoes. She picks up a shoe and feels its shape. We understand that she is blind. She begins to weep quietly, drops the shoe and exits.* ALBERTINA *sits up on the bed. There is a yellow smile on her face.*

Blackout.

Music: Portuguese guitar; a plaintive fado instrumental plays through the next scene.

Scene 2 Later that night

The lights come up to reveal the empty bedroom. The bedding is rumpled. Inês enters and moves towards the bed. She reaches out and smoothes the wrinkles in the bedspread. She picks up a pillow, draws it to her face and reacts to Albertina's smell. Custódio appears in the doorway. He watches as Inês changes the pillow cover.

Fade to black as music ends.

Scene 3 One year later

Albertina is giving birth to Anita. Dona Rosa and Dona Eugénia are the midwives. Dona Rosa wipes the sweat from Albertina's brow. Dona Eugénia grumbles.

D. Rosa:

Vá lá Dona Albertina, mais um bocadinho. Está quase.

D. Eugénia:

This isn't your first child. You know what to do.

Albertina:

Meu Deus . . . Nossa Senhora cheia de graça . . .

D. Eugénia:

Now she prays!

D. Rosa:

Ela pensa que vai morrer, coitada.

D. Eugénia:

If she's worried about dying she should have thought of that nine months ago!

ALBERTINA:

Mandem chamar o Padre António . . .

D. EUGÉNIA:

Father António? You know what he thinks of all this. He won't even baptize the child!

D. ROSA:

Coitada. Ficou viúva e agora isto.

D. EUGÉNIA:

A widow in mourning bearing a child. A child that is not her husband's. I heard she's put little Mário in an orphanage.

D. ROSA:

O filho dela ficou sem o pai, coitadinho.

ALBERTINA:

Ajudai-me Senhor . . .

D. EUGÉNIA:

And now she's bringing another fatherless child into the world. Will this one go to the orphanage too?

D. ROSA:

Dizem que ele, o amante, vem cá p'ra casa.

D. EUGÉNIA:

He's moving in here? He's leaving his blind wife?

ALBERTINA:

Perdoai-me Senhor . . .

Scene 4   1950, kitchen.

A water whistle imitates a nightingale.

Music: a children's song played on a recorder or flute.

Lights up on ten-year-old ANITA. *She is at a table copying out the times table. She looks around, gets up, opens a drawer and removes a stack of magazines. They are* fotonovelas, *photo-stories of love, jealousy and revenge. She goes back to the table and shoves her workbooks out of the way. She opens each magazine to the back page and separates the pile in two. One pile has stories that end in a wedding; the other pile has stories that end in a kiss.*

ANITA:

Beijinho. Beijinho. Casamento. Casamento. Casamento. Beijinho. Casamento. Beijinho . . .

From the drawer, ANITA *removes a small object wrapped in tissue. She gets a loaf of bread from the bread box. She unwraps a plastic bride and groom and places them on top of the bread. With a tea towel on her head like a veil she stands in front of a mirror singing.*

ANITA:

Já passei a roupa a ferro
Já passei o meu vestido
Amanhã vou-me casar
O Manel é meu marido

DONA ROSA *and* DONA EUGÉNIA *join her in the song. In the following dialogue, some of their lines overlap.*

D. ROSA:

O sonho de todas as raparigas é ir de véu e grinalda.

D. Eugénia:

Lots of lace and a very long train.

D. Rosa:

É o dia mais bonito na vida de uma mulher.

D. Eugénia:

Such a special day! And then a little house with lace curtains in the windows.

D. Rosa:

Toalhas de mesa bordadas com naperons iguais.

D. Eugénia:

Matching doilies.

D. Rosa:

Um mimo! Tudo limpinho.

D. Eugénia:

Ah yes! A spotless house is everything. And children!

D. Rosa:

Criancinhas. As meninas de trancinhas e os rapazes a jogar à bola . . .

D. Eugénia:

It's a dream come true!

D. Rosa:

Um sonho . . .

D. Eugénia:

A dream . . .

D. Rosa:

Um sonho . . .

D. Eugénia:

A dream . . .

Anita dreams of her wedding day. The Musician plays the adufe while the other actors dance around Anita. They are holding wedding dresses as they would partners.

Musician:

Cravo roxo à janela
É sinal de casamento
Menina recolha o cravo, ó aí
Que o casar 'inda tem tempo

The wedding dress dance ends. Albertina talks to Dona Rosa and Mário to Dona Eugénia. They are in different places, but intercutting each other's speeches in time.

Albertina:

Cá vou indo, uns dias melhores outros piores. O Custódio é que piora todos os dias. Desde que se reformou passa todo o santo dia de na cama e a resmungar. A mulher dele é que tem a obrigação de aturá-lo na velhice.

Mário:

My so-called stepfather is going back to live with his wife.

Albertina:

Quando o Custódio se for embora, o Mário pode viver connosco. Já acabou o curso da Casa Pia e vai arranjar um bom trabalho. Como filho mais velho, será o chefe de família.

Mário:

I'll have to support my mother and Anita.

Albertina:

O ordenado do meu Mário será superior à reforma miserável do Custódio.

MÁRIO:

I don't mind taking care of Anita. She's a good girl.

ALBERTINA:

E a Anita gosta muito do irmão. Nem sentirá a falta do pai.

MÁRIO:

I think she'll miss her father.

Scene 5   1960, bedroom and kitchen

Music: Portuguese guitar, a sad melody, plays through the next scene.

ANITA and VICTOR are in the bedroom, talking with strained pauses.
ALBERTINA in kitchen, eavesdropping.

ANITA:

The doctor says I should think of leaving the factory. I could do some sewing work at home. All the neighbours say my dresses are perfectly made. I'll soon be well. It was only a fall.

VICTOR:

Acho que devíamos adiar a data do casamento.

ANITA:

But the dress is almost ready.

VICTOR:

Sem o teu ordenado da fábrica vai ser difícil. Vou ter que trabalhar aos Sábados. Os meus pais já andam a chatear . . .

ANITA:

You're breaking off our engagement.

VICTOR:

Sim. Tem que ser. As melhoras.

Music changes to a quicker tempo as VICTOR *exits in a hurry but* ALBERTINA *stands in his way; she smiles and shakes his hand, then turns him around and pats him on the back, encouraging him to leave.*

ALBERTINA:

Adeus, Senhor Victor.

VICTOR:

Dona Albertina—

ALBERTINA:

Boa tarde, Senhor Victor. Com licença.

ALBERTINA exits. VICTOR *stands for a moment hesitating, then exits.* DONA ROSA *and* DONA EUGÉNIA *enter.*

D. EUGÉNIA:

Anita is ill, poor thing.

D. ROSA:

Coitada, teve um acidente e ficou de cama.

D. EUGÉNIA:

It was a fall. She fell at the factory and had a . . . something happened to her, she had a . . . she had a fit. It was ugly. Poor thing.

D. ROSA:

Coitada. A queda deu-lhe cabo da saúde. Não poderá ter uma vida normal.

D. EUGÉNIA:

No. Victor has broken off the engagement! He wants a healthy normal girl for a wife. Poor Anita. Poor thing.

D. Rosa:

Coitada. E se tivesse filhos e se acontecesse alguma coisa aos filhos.

D. Eugénia:

It would be terrible if they had children. She'll have to live with her mother and brother for the rest of her life, poor thing.

D. Rosa:

Coitada. Já não pode trabalhar. Mas ouvi dizer que o irmão, o Mário, vai emigrar.

D. Eugénia:

Mário? Where is he going?

D. Rosa:

P'ro Canadá.

D. Eugénia:

To Canada?

D. Rosa:

A Anita vai ficar sozinha com a mãe. Coitada.

D. Eugénia:

Poor thing. Victor left (*flying away gesture*).

D. Rosa:

E o Mário vai-se embora (*flying away gesture*).

D. Eugénia and D. Rosa:

Poor thing! / Coitada!

Blackout.

Scene 6   A few months later, kitchen.

MUSICIAN:

Vou-me embora, vou partir, mas tenho esperança
De correr o mundo inteiro, quero ir
Quero ver e conhecer rosa branca
E a vida dum marinheiro sem dormir

> *By the table there is an open trunk. On the table there is a neat pile of clothes, toiletry items, books, tools and a small, open suitcase. MÁRIO enters with some clean, ironed shirts and places them in the trunk. He places some items in the suitcase, packing in a neat, orderly manner. Sometimes he refolds a piece of clothing or dusts off a book before packing it. ALBERTINA and ANITA stand at the opposite end of the stage watching MÁRIO. ALBERTINA has her arm through ANITA's and she looks self-satisfied. ANITA looks stricken, trying not to cry. She tries to move to MÁRIO but ALBERTINA strengthens her grip. This happens three times. MÁRIO does not acknowledge their presence, he just keeps packing.*

> *Lights fade as music ends.*

Scene 7   Lisboa and Toronto, 1960 to 1975

> *In two distinct areas, ALBERTINA and ANITA's home in Lisboa and MÁRIO's room in Toronto, the following actions a) and a), b) and b), and so on to g) and g) happen simultaneously. Parts of each scene will pull focus at different times but there is a careful choreography that matches the movements on the opposite sides of the stage. There is a voiceover of phrases from letters.* Portuguese guitar music cues the beginning and end of each scene.*

* Lisboa VO:

Querido filho, Querido irmão, Filho, Espero que esta carta te encontre de saúde que nós por cá vamos bem. Recebemos a tua carta de . . . Com um abraço da mãe e muitas saudades da mana que nunca te esquece.

* Toronto VO:

Mãe, Querida mãe e irmã, Espero que esta carta a encontre de saúde em companhia da Anita. Peço desculpa de não ter escrito antes. Um abraço. Beijinhos da Teresa e da Susana.

a) ANITA and ALBERTINA are at the kitchen table. ANITA writes while ALBERTINA dictates. When ALBERTINA is finished, she gets up businesslike and starts preparing a meal. ANITA adds a few lines to the letter and seals it with a tear in her eye.

a) MÁRIO is sitting on a cot. He arranges the bedside table so he can write on it. He takes a letter from the drawer, reads it quickly and begins to write. Before sealing the letter, he takes a money order from his wallet and puts it in the envelope.

b) CARLOS delivers a registered letter. ANITA signs for it. ALBERTINA removes the money order and hands the letter to ANITA. ALBERTINA rushes CARLOS away as she leaves; ANITA reads the letter.

b) MÁRIO is lying on the cot reading a letter. He puts it down and picks up a book. He is restless and bored. He gets up and bundles up to go outside.

c) CARLOS delivers another letter. ANITA signs for it, and reads as CARLOS watches her. He asks for a glass of water. ANITA brings him a glass of wine and invites him to sit at the table. CARLOS toasts

ANITA. *She smiles at him. He leans towards her.* ALBERTINA *enters, looks at them disapprovingly and rushes* CARLOS *out.*

c) TERESA *hands* MÁRIO *a present. He opens it.* MÁRIO *kisses* TERESA. *He gets her a chair and invites her to sit.* MÁRIO *brings out a chess game.* TERESA *makes a move. They smile at each other in between chess moves.*

d) ANITA *and* CARLOS *at the table.* CARLOS *finishes his wine.* ANITA *gets up to get more wine.* CARLOS *takes her hand and proposes.* ANITA *pulls back and shakes her head no.* CARLOS *puts on his cap.*

d) MÁRIO *and* TERESA *are sitting on the cot.* TERESA *laughs. She gets up and reaches for her coat.* MÁRIO *takes her hand and proposes.* TERESA *nods yes. They kiss.*

ALBERTINA *stands centre stage and views the frozen tableaus of the two previous scenes; she is obviously pleased with both situations.*

Music: "Desta Vida Fiz um Xaile"

e) ANITA *is ill and wrapped in a shawl. She is dressing a doll with a baby outfit. She holds it lovingly. She has an epileptic seizure.* ALBERTINA *rushes in and shoves a rolled-up facecloth between her teeth. She tries to hold her down as the convulsions get more violent.*

e) TERESA *is holding a baby.* MÁRIO *enters with a parcel. They open it and find baby clothes made by* ANITA *and a rattle.* MÁRIO *waves the rattle at the baby.* TERESA *smiles.*

f) ANITA *is reading a* fotonovela. ALBERTINA *brings in a framed photo of* SUSANA. ANITA *holds the photo lovingly.*

f) MÁRIO *is reading to his seven-year-old daughter* SUSANA *who is wearing a dress like* ANITA'S *doll's.* MÁRIO *leaves and* SUSANA *takes a few* fotonovelas *from under the bed and looks through them delightedly.*

g) ANITA *enters with a bunch of red carnations and puts them in a vase. Albertina smiles wryly.*

g) MÁRIO *is reading a Portuguese newspaper. He is moved by the news of the Revolution of the Carnations. He hugs* TERESA *and* SUSANA *ecstatically.*

By the end of sequence g), the music has sped up as the actors rush to create a tableau of revolutionary joy. MUSICIAN *sings "Grândola, Vila Morena."* SUSANA *reads a letter to* ANITA.

SUSANA:

Dear Tia Anita. Hi. I hope you and Avozinha are fine. I'm fine thank you. My dad is writing in Portuguese while I tell him what to say in English. He says that I have to learn to write in Portuguese too but I can't even speak it too well. My dad is really happy about 25 de Abril and I even saw him cry. Thank you for the magazines you sent me. I love them! I love looking at the pictures. Do you have a boyfriend? Are you getting married? My dad says you're too sick. Are you in the hospital? Please write soon, OK? Lots of kisses and saudades for you and Avozinha from Susana.

Scene 8   Lisboa, 1976

ANITA is at the sewing machine with white tulle in clouds around her.
She reads aloud.

ANITA:

My dearest Anita, I read your letter with joy. Many people told me to be patient, and they were right. Can it be true? Have you accepted my proposal after all these years? I am so happy. I will come to Lisboa during my holidays. We can be married and you then can come with me to France. With all my love, Carlos.

ANITA picks up a wedding dress and dances with it humming, "Já passei
a roupa a ferro." DONA ROSA and DONA EUGÉNIA appear.

D. EUGÉNIA:

All these years Anita's been making wedding dresses for young girls.

D. ROSA:

O trabalho dela é muito perfeitinho. Já vestiu tantas noivas.

D. EUGÉNIA:

And now? She's getting married herself!

D. ROSA:

Casar-se com esta idade! Será que vai de véu e grinalda?

D. EUGÉNIA:

No, no, no, she's too old for a traditional wedding dress and veil. A nice beige suit with a modest hat. Carlos will like that.

D. ROSA:

O Carlos, depois de tantos anos. Dizem que enviuvou lá p'ra França.

D. Eugénia:

Yes, he's a widower now and remembered Anita, his first love. Dona Albertina doesn't know yet!

D. Rosa:

A Dona Albertina ainda não sabe.

D. Eugénia:

Dona Albertina doesn't know yet?

> Dona Eugénia *and* Dona Rosa *whisper their lines and circle* Anita. Anita *holds the letter to her heart as the lights fade.*

Scene 9   A week later

> Anita *is sewing a lady's suit with beige material.* Albertina *is darning socks.*

Albertina:

Estou aflita da vista. É assim depois duma certa idade. Até tu vais precisar de óculos se continuas a cansar a vista dessa maneira. Nem sabes o que te espera. Também fui nova e não me preocupava com nada. Agora nem tenho paciência p'ra remendar estas meias—ai, quem me dera ter vinte anos! E ter saúde—a saúde é tudo. Tu tiveste pouca sorte Anita, paciência.

> *There is a knock on the door.* Anita *lets* Inês *in.* Albertina *reacts with surprise and hostility. During* Inês's *long speech she echoes some phrases, remembering.* Anita *listens and weeps.*

Albertina:

O que é que você quer?

Inês:

That voice. Your terrible voice. After all these years it still chills me to the bone.

Albertina:

O que quer de mim?

Inês:

I have come to set things right. Custódio is dead. The lady who opened the door must be your daughter. Let me see, she would be thirty-four years old now. Anita. Custódio remembered her often, spoke her name.

Anita:

My father.

Inês:

Yes. Anita's father. Custódio remembered Anita and I remember you, Albertina. Ah yes, time goes by and I can't forget you, Albertina. Sometimes I forget if I've had lunch or if I've taken my pills but I can't forget the first night that I heard your laughter in my house. I was in bed. My sheets smelled of lavender. I keep lavender sprigs in the linen drawers. I was waiting for Custódio to come home. I heard his key in the door and then, strangely enough, I heard him speak softly. He bumped against the sofa and you laughed. Then you began. The sofa springs were old and rusty. I heard you say, "No, stop, I can't with her in the house." But you came back when I wasn't home. And then, one winter afternoon, it was dark at six o'clock, I came home from the shopping and I heard you in the bedroom. In my bedroom. When Custódio had his pleasure I heard his usual grunt. I walked in and asked who was with him. I don't know how I had the courage. But he said he was just napping, got up and left the room. I stayed. You also stayed, perhaps thinking that I didn't know you were there. Do you remember that I tried to reach the bed but tripped on a shoe? I picked it up. It wasn't Custódio's or mine. It had a chunky heel. It was yours. Then I started to cry. I was young then. What shame I felt! Yes. I felt shame. But not anymore. When Custódio died, my shame died with him. Custódio denied ever having a child with you. But your daughter, who weeps for her dead father, or maybe for you, Albertina, has used my husband's name all her life. She should know the truth, shouldn't she? That my husband never gave her his name. I don't know if these things matter anymore but Anita should know that she's illegitimate. And she should know that her mother is a whore. That's all I came for. Please show me to the door.

Inês exits. Albertina sits stone-faced. Anita is crying softly. She takes Carlos' letter from her bosom and reads it aloud. Albertina takes the letter and rips it in two.

ALBERTINA:

Não, Anita, não te vais casar e não vais p'ra França. Vens comigo para o Canadá e para ao pé do teu irmão. Sacrifiquei a minha vida por ti. Não me podes abandonar.

ANITA:

Please, mother, please let me go.

ALBERTINA:

Nunca. Pensas que és alguma garota de dezasseis anos, a preparar-se p'ra fugir com o namoradinho? Coitada, a vida não é como nas novelas. É o que viste agora. Pensas que o Carlos esperou por ti? Foi casado. Um homem não consegue viver sozinho, precisa duma mulher p'ra lhe lavar as cuecas. E agora tu é que vais fazer a lida da casa dele? Uma rapariga doente como tu, Anita? Não te iludas! Podes piorar dum dia p'ro outro. Até podes ficar de cama durante meses. Achas que o Carlos vai aguentar isso? O teu pai não aguentou viver com uma cega. Os homens são todos iguais. Anita, o teu irmão está farto de nos pedir p'ra ir p'ro pé dele. E tu gostas tanto da Susana—da Xaninha, seria a tua felicidade, Anita. vamos, filha, vamos para o Canadá. O Mário, a Susana, o Canadá. O Canadá.

As ALBERTINA *dreams of a new life in Canada, a light comes up on* MÁRIO *in Toronto.*

MÁRIO:

I arrived in Toronto fifteen years ago. I didn't mean to make my life here. Only a few years, only a few years to save up some money and go back home. Now that fascism is dead I could return and have a decent life in Lisboa. A new democracy, a new economy, a chance for the working class. But I have a family here, Teresa, my daughter Susana. Susana doesn't speak Portuguese. How would she handle school there? We have a life here. And my mother and Anita want to join us. Then we'll all be here. There'll be no reason to return. We'll go for holidays. It's what everybody ends up doing.

MUSICIAN sings:

Todas numa carreirinha
As estrelas do céu correm
Aí, todas numa carreirinha
Todas numa carreirinha
Assim corressem amores
Da vossa mão para a minha

During the song, ALBERTINA *and* ANITA *pack, say goodbye to the neighbours and move to Canada.*

D. ROSA:

E a Anita lá foi com a mãe para o Canadá. Rompeu o noivado com o Carlos.

D. Eugénia:

Albertina sacrificed her life for Anita. It's Anita's duty to stay with her mother.

D. Rosa:

Coitada da Anita. Nunca irá vestida de véu e grinalda.

D. Eugénia:

She's almost forty. She's old and sick. What does she expect?

D. Rosa:

Era o sonho dela.

D. Eugénia:

Dreams? Dreams! What good are dreams? Health is everything.

Scene 10   Toronto 1976

Susana's bedroom. Anita and Susana are looking at a snapshots kept in a shoebox. Anita sings.

Anita:

"Sapateia, meu bem sapateia, ai vira e volta à sapateia" and when they danced, all the girls looked like bells swaying back and forth. I made some of these costumes for the parades in June. And at Carnaval I made the costumes for the boys and girls on our street. I really liked making the girls' costumes—fairies, witches, princesses, and even some traditional costumes like on that doll I sent you for your eighth birthday. A fisherwoman from Nazaré.

Susana hands the Nazaré doll to Anita.

ANITA:

See? Six petticoats, a skirt and an apron. I sewed the lace on the petticoats and embroidered the apron. Look, she has real underclothes—panties and a bra.

SUSANA:

Yeah, she's pretty. Bonito.

ANITA:

Bonita. Sim, bonita. Como tu, querida. Pretty, just like you.

SUSANA:

Tia, when I was little you used to make my baby clothes, right?

ANITA:

Sim, sim querida. I liked making baby clothes—and if you hadn't been so far away I would've made all your little dresses. I also liked making doll clothes. I dressed up big dolls and sat them on the bed like princesses. They looked so pretty, like little girls with ringlets. Like my little girls.

(ANITA *starts to cry softly.*)

SUSANA:

Tia, what's the matter? Are you OK?

ANITA:

Sim, sim, estou OK. I had so many dreams before. Even after that first day that I fell at the factory. I still dreamed I would get married and have children. I wasn't that sick. And when I came to Canada I felt a little stronger—I thought I would get much better and meet different people, Canadian people, maybe a Canadian gentleman who would want to marry me. But I only know other Portuguese people and they're even worse here. They're so judgmental, cruel even. No, it's not them—it's me,

I'm just old and weak. I'll never marry and have children—not in Lisbon, not in Toronto, nowhere. I have no more dreams.

Scene 11   Living room.

ALBERTINA, ANITA *and* SUSANA *are watching a soap opera,* General Hospital. ANITA *and* ALBERTINA *are sitting on the couch.* SUSANA *is sitting cross-legged on the floor eating chips.*

ALBERTINA:

Não percebo nada. A televisão está para aí ligada o dia inteiro e não se percebe nada. É só para os Canadianos.

ANITA:

Mãe, assim a menina não ouve nada.

ALBERTINA:

Ora essa! Se pelo menos soubesse explicar o que se passa nesses programas mas nem uma palavra de português sai daquela boquinha. Não é minha menina? Dizes que percebes tudo mas a Avó não acredita.

SUSANA:

I do so understand. And stop buggin' me to speak Portuguese already.

ALBERTINA:

Já se viu uma neta responder dessa maneira à Avó? Ainda levas—

ANITA:

Xaninha anda cá p'ro colo da tia, querida.

SUSANA:

Holy cow! I'm too old to sit on your lap. Leave me alone. Can't you see I'm watching *General Hospital*?

ALBERTINA:

Agora fica aí agarrada a ver publicidade. De cinco em cinco minutos aparece um parvo qualquer a querer vender uma porcaria qualquer e depois nós é que temos que aturar os miúdos no supermercado. Isto é que é um martírio! E quando penso que o teu irmão só come sandes ao almoço e à pressa. Isto só visto. Só no Canadá.

ANITA:

Quando acabar a novela vou descascar as batatas.

ALBERTINA:

E a Susana vai ajudar a tia.

SUSANA:

I have homework to do. No posso peel the potatoes.

ALBERTINA:

Não podes? Quais não podes, és aleijadinha? Se eu fosse a tua mãe—

ALBERTINA *exits shaking her head. The commercials are over and the soap opera continues.*

ANITA:

Susana, vem p'ra aqui p'ro pé da tia.

ANITA:

Susana, tu já tens um namorado, não é filha? Esse menino que vem cá de bicicleta.

SUSANA:

He's not my boyfriend, Tia! I just like him. Gosta ele.

ANITA:

Gostas dele? E de certeza que ele também gosta de ti. Como é que ele se chama?

SUSANA:

Martín.

ANITA:

Mórteen?

SUSANA:

Mar-tín.

ANITA:

Mar-tín.

SUSANA:

Right! I knew you could say it right. Tia, you're gonna learn how to speak
English and then we're gonna find you a boyfriend! Like him!

*SUSANA points at the TV and they giggle. SUSANA makes a smooch-
ing sound at the TV. ANITA copies her and they giggle some more.
MÁRIO appears in the doorway and watches them. ALBERTINA enters
from the kitchen and also watches them. She and MÁRIO exchange a
look. The lights go down slowly.*

Scene 12

DONA ROSA and DONA EUGÉNIA's commentary.

D. ROSA:

Está tão doente, não pode passear sozinha.

D. EUGÉNIA:

I always see her with her mother. Can't she go out alone anymore?

D. ROSA:

A Anita gosta muito da sobrinha, da Susana.

D. Eugénia:

Her niece is like a daughter to her. People say she still thinks of getting married.

D. Rosa:

Casar? Não há homem que queira uma rapariga doente. A Anita teve pouca sorte.

D. Eugénia:

She's fine just as she is. She's with her mother, her brother, her darling niece.

D. Rosa:

Pois é! Assim é que está bem.

D. Eugénia:

She's fine just as she is!

Scene 13   A few months later. Department store.

> Anita, Albertina and Susana are browsing in the perfume section of a large department store. Susana gets Anita to try on some perfume. Albertina doesn't like this. Susana leads the way to the escalator and is about to go up when her grandmother stops her.

Albertina:

Esperem. Esperem por mim. Susana! Espera aí! A tua tia não pode subir por aí, vamos procurar as escadas.

Anita:

Que parvoíce! Vamos por aqui que a Susana sabe onde vai.

Susana:

What's goin' on?

ALBERTINA:

A tua tia não pode subir nessas escadas que pode-lhe dar alguma coisa. Anita, vê lá onde te metes—ficas toda nervosa e podes tropeçar—às tantas ficas para aí estendida e depois? Isto não é Portugal, mandam-te logo para o hospital.

SUSANA:

Avó, nothing's gonna happen to Tia. It's only an escalator. Nunca andas num escada assim?

ANITA:

Não, sobrinha, a Avó pensa que eu sou uma criança que não aguento uma brincadeira dessas.

ALBERTINA:

Anita, é verdade que o teu coração não aguenta! Não digas que não é verdade. Anda daí e vamos procurar as escadas e subir devagarinho.

SUSANA:

Avozinha, it's OK. Come on Tia, you go first and I'll go behind you in case you trip. Vai na frente. Come on, it's easy.

ALBERTINA:

Anita, não te atrevas. Não faças isso, Anita.

SUSANA:

Come on! It's not a big deal!

>   SUSANA *steps onto the escalator but* ANITA *and* ALBERTINA *stay behind.* ALBERTINA *starts to walk away.* ANITA *stares up at* SUSANA *who beckons for her to follow.* ANITA *doesn't move.*

>   *Music:* adufe *and* trancanholas *play a percussive beat.*

*Anita wanders slowly into a spot, and steps up onto a low pedestal.
Susana, Albertina, Mário, Inês, Custódio, Dona
Rosa, Dona Eugénia, and Victor approach Anita. Each has
a piece of a wedding dress that they pin to her clothes. Finally, Anita
is standing dressed as a bride. Albertina closes Anita's eyes and
arranges her arms as in death. Dona Rosa and Dona Eugénia
step into the spot, dressed as mourners.*

D. Rosa:

Coitada, era tão nova.

D. Eugénia:

Only forty years old. And she didn't die of those fits. Imagine, it was her heart.

D. Rosa:

Foi o coração. A Dona Albertina teve o desgosto de ver a filha morrer. Que tristeza.

D. Eugénia:

It was God's will. There's nothing to be done.

D. Rosa:

O destino. É o destino.

D. Eugénia:

Doesn't she look beautiful though?

D. Rosa:

É verdade, está muito bonita.

*A wailing is heard. Lights up to show Mário in a black suit, Susana
in a dark dress holding his hand. Albertina is at the opposite end of
the stage in deep mourning. A group of women in black shawls kneel near*

ANITA. *They are* carpideiras, *praying for the soul of the dead. It is clear that* ANITA *is in her coffin dressed as a bride.*

Music: a plaintive fado instrumental.

Lights fade slowly to black.

BIOGRAPHICAL NOTES

Clemente Alves was born on the island of São Jorge in the Azores. His family immigrated to Canada in 1974 where they settled in Toronto's Little Portugal. He studied theatre arts, film and television production. In the mid-90s, he founded the infamous cowpunk band, The Yeehaa Cowboys, released an album of originals, and co-wrote and starred in the stage musical of the same name. At the age of twenty-eight, he left Canada for a grand adventure through Europe with the idea of returning home after experiencing Euro 2004 in Lisbon, but he never made it back. In 2008 he was film editor on the documentary *Taking the Face: The Portuguese Bullfight* which premiered at the Artivist Film Festival. Alves currently works for MTV Networks in Portugal.

Edith Baguinho has been greatly shaped and influenced by both Portuguese and Canadian landscapes. Her poetry and articles have appeared in community newspapers (*The Kensington* and *The Harbourfront Outlook*), literary and art publications (*Y.U.P.A. Voice, Icon Magazine,* and *The New Muse of Contempt*), and online (*P.E.V., Bloor Street News,* and *Poetry Expresso Café*). She has one book in print, *Ode to Tio Caliço and Tia Dores* (Exile Editions, 1997). Baguinho creates and posts her most recent and experimental work on her website, *Poetry Expresso Café*. Born and currently living in Toronto, she divides her time between Canada and Portugal.

Nelia Botelho is a poet of Azorean descent, born and raised in Vancouver, British Columbia. She earned a BA in Creative Writing and English from Kwantlen Polytechnic University and studied poetry at the Banff Centre.

Esmeralda Cabral is a graduate of The Writer's Studio at Simon Fraser University and is currently working on a series of family stories. Her work has been published in several anthologies, magazines, and in *The Globe and Mail*. Two of her stories have aired on CBC Radio. Esmeralda lives and writes in Vancouver.

Tony Correia is the author of the book, *Foodsluts at Doll & Penny's Café*. His essays have appeared in *The Globe & Mail*, *Vancouver Review*, *SubTerrain*, *SAD Mag*, *T(our)* as well as several anthologies. Correia has been a columnist and contributor to *Xtra* in Vancouver since 2006.

paulo da costa was born in Angola and raised in Portugal. He is a bilingual writer, editor and translator living on the West Coast of Canada. His first book of fiction, *The Scent of a Lie*, received the Commonwealth First Book Prize (Canada and Caribbean region) and the W.O. Mitchell City of Calgary Book Prize. His poetry and fiction have been published in literary magazines around the world and have been translated into Italian, Chinese, Spanish, Serbian, Slovenian, and Portuguese. His latest book of fiction, *The Green and Purple Skin of the World*, was released by Freehand Books (Broadview Press) in 2013.

Humberto da Silva is a Toronto boy, born and bred. During completion of the 4th grade in fascist Portugal he discovered through the study of history that Sir Francis Drake was a thieving pirate and that the Portuguese were the first to fly across the Atlantic. A desire to conquer the English language resulted in literary pretensions and numerous short story publications. The inclusion of "Compassion Fatigue" in *Best Canadian Stories 92* (Oberon Press) was a high point in his existence. Da Silva is an award-winning videographer, a citizen journalist, and a radical commentator for rabble.ca. Recently he was vilified nationally for transgressing Godwin's Law. His day job is working as a union representative. He lives, of course, in Toronto, in an empty nest with his beloved wife Lina da Silva, nee da Silva, and his cat Silver.

Aida Jordão is an actor, director, playwright, and scholar committed to feminist performance, applied theatre, and Portuguese Canadian projects. For thirty years, Jordão has worked with both professional theatre workers and community partici- pants worldwide to devise original political theatre: in Toronto with Nightwood Theatre, Ground Zero Productions, and the Company of Sirens, and abroad in

Portugal, Nicaragua, and Cuba. She holds an Acting Diploma from the Drama Studio, U.K., and an M.A. in Drama, from the University of Toronto. Jordão is a course instructor at the University of Toronto and York University and is currently a Ph.D. candidate at the Centre for Drama, Theatre and Performance Studies, University of Toronto, with the thesis, "Inês de Castro in Theatre and Film: A Feminist Exhumation of the Dead Queen."

Irene Marques holds a Ph.D. in Comparative Literature, a Masters in French Literature, a Masters in Comparative Literature and a Bachelor of Social Work. She is a bilingual writer (English and Portuguese), has taught African and Caribbean literatures, comparative and world literature, literary theory, writing and rhetoric and Portuguese at the Ontario College of Art and Design University and the University of Toronto for over ten years. Her academic publications include the manuscripts *The Works of Chin Ce: A Critical Overview* (2007), *Transnational Discourses on Class, Gender and Cultural Identity* (2012) and numerous articles in international journals including *African Identities: Journal of Economics, Culture and Society, Research in African Literatures,* and *CLCWeb: Comparative Literature and Culture.* She is the author of a short story collection, *Habitando na Metáfora do Tempo: Crónicas Desejadas* (Dwelling in the Metaphor of Time: Desired Chronicles), as well as the poetry collections, *Wearing Glasses of Water, The Perfect Unravelling of the Spirit and the Circular Incantation: An Exercise in Loss and Findings.* Her novel *My House is a Mansion* will be published by Leaping Lyon Books (York University) in 2015. She emigrated from Portugal to Canada at the age of twenty and lives in Toronto where she currently teaches in the English Department at Ryerson University and in the Department of Languages, Literatures and Linguistics at York University.

Antonio M. Marques has short stories, essays and poems published in magazines and anthologies including the *Core, Muse Journal, Alias, Open Door Magazine, Tidepool 9, Subtle Fires, Canadian Writer's Journal.* His work has also been published in the book, *Magical Motherhood,* and in the *Newsletter of the Literary Arts and*

Humanities of the School for Spiritual Science in North America. Marques is compiling a book on poetry and its inner sources with excerpts from Rudolf Steiner's works. He lives in Don Mills, Ontario.

Emanuel Melo was born on the island of São Miguel in the Azores and immigrated to Canada at the age of nine. His articles have appeared in the magazine *TWAS* (*Toronto World Arts Scene*) and on the website of the Canadian Centre for Azorean Research and Studies. His story, "Avó Lives Alone," was a finalist in the Writers' Union of Canada 20th Annual Short Prose Competition for Developing Writers in 2013. He is currently working on a collection of short stories that draws on his Portuguese Canadian heritage. He lives in Toronto.

Eduardo Bettencourt Pinto was born in Gabela, Angola in 1954 and has lived in Canada since 1983. He has published several books of poetry and fiction. His most recent books include a collection of bilingual (English and Portuguese) poetry, *Travelling with Shadows* (2008), a poetry collection in Portuguese, *A Cor do Sul nos teus Olhos* (2012), and a work of fiction in chapbook format, *Aubrianne* (2013). He is represented in several anthologies and collective books in Portugal, Angola, Brazil, England, United States, Canada, Latvia, Italy, and Cuba. Pinto lives in Pitt Meadows, British Columbia.

Paul Serralheiro was born in Riba Fria, Portugal, in 1956 and moved to Montréal with his family in 1959. A student of literature and music at Concordia University (B.A., B.F.A., M.A.), Serralheiro has worked as a journalist (print and radio), as a guitarist and trumpeter, and as a teacher of English in schools in Montréal, Toronto and Vancouver. His poetry has appeared in several journals including *Arc*, *Antigonish Review*, *Event*, and *Zymergy*, and an anthology (*Buda Books Poetry Series*). He lives in Montréal where he works as an English professor at Dawson College and plays trumpet in the free jazz quartet Shortest Longest Day.

Richard Simas is a freelance writer with a background in literature, music, and the performing arts, contributing regularly to contemporary arts and literary reviews. His work has been published in Europe and in North America, including the *Journey Prize Stories* anthology, and his fiction won a Fiddlehead literary prize. He is a frequent collaborator for Toronto's *Musicworks* magazine. Thanks to an award from Portugal's Camoes Institute in 2011, Simas attended the Disquiet International Literary Program in Lisbon. In 1990, Simas founded Théâtre La Chapelle in Montréal, an interdisciplinary performing centre dedicated to experimentation. He currently performs with a nine-member street band named Valody whose New Music-Spoken Word performance based on Fernando Pessoa's *Book of Disquiet* premiered at the Open Ears Festival in Kitchener, Ontario. Simas lives in Montréal, Québec.

Laureano Soares was born in the village of Sobral de São Miguel in Covilhã, Portugal. He emigrated from Portugal to Canada at the age of nineteen and writes in both Portuguese and French. His poems have appeared in the poetry review, *Carquois,* and in a literary anthology published by the Cercle des Poètes de la Montérégie. His most recent book, *Imagens do Coração* (2012) is trilingual: Portuguese, Spanish and French. Soares is an active member of a neighbourhood *tertúlia* (literary salon) which includes writers and artists of Portuguese, French and Spanish ethnicity. He lives in Montréal, Québec.

EDITORIAL BOARD

María João Dodman is Assistant Professor of Portuguese Studies at York University's Department of Languages, Literatures and Linguistics. She is a native of the Azores, Portugal, and she has lived in Canada since 1989. She specializes in early modern Spanish and Portuguese literature. She is co-chair of the Canadian Centre for Azorean Research and Studies (CCARS) and a member of the

Advisory Council of the Consulate of Portugal in Toronto. Currently, Dr. Dodman is researching the concept of Açorianidade (Azoreanness) and its manifestations not only in the literature produced in the region of the Azores, but also in the Diaspora.

Hugh Hazelton is a writer and translator who specializes in the comparison of Canadian and Quebec literatures with those of Latin America, as well as in Quebec poetry and the work of Latin American writers of Canada. He has written four books of poetry and translates from Spanish, French, and Portuguese into English; his translation of *Vétiver* (Signature, 2005), a book of poems by Joël Des Rosiers, won the Governor General's award for French-English translation in 2006. His book *Latinocanadá: A Critical Study of Ten Latin American Writers of Canada* (McGill-Queen's, 2007) received the Best Book award from the Canadian Association of Hispanists for the period 2007–2009. He is a professor emeritus of Spanish at Concordia University in Montreal and now works as co-director of the Banff International Literary Translation Centre.

Fernanda Viveiros is the publisher of Fidalgo Books, an independent press dedicated to publishing writers of Portuguese ethnicity and books in translation. She is the former producer of the BC Book Prizes and Word On The Street Vancouver, and served as the executive director of the Federation of BC Writers from 2006– 2008. Viveiros divides her time between Vancouver, British Columbia, and Bellingham, Washington, where she currently resides with her family.